More Praise for *The Right Way of Death*

"Whether you are an interested bystander, a seasoned professional, or just getting started in our great industry, I wholeheartedly recommend *The Right Way of Death*. Its message clarifies who we are but also who we can be for the families we serve."

—Robert A. Gordon Jr., President and CEO,
Cypress Lawn Cemetery, California

"The ideas in this book have challenged me to change my thinking. I can see that I need to realign our business practices with what consumers genuinely value. Laying aside assumptions, delving deeply into the truths of life, of death, and consumer experiences, Eric Layer brings a brilliant analysis of how to truly market and promote what we do. Using his approach, we will disrupt our own businesses for the good of our customers, our companies, and our employees."

—Brad Speaks, President and CEO, Speaks Chapels, Missouri

"A fascinating read. Layer has brilliantly captured both the troubled history and the current challenges of the death care profession. He has given us exactly what we needed—a pat on the back and a kick in the tail."

—Gary Freytag, President and CEO,
Spring Grove Cemetery and Arboretum, Ohio

"It is rare that a book comes along that forces us to ask important and challenging questions of ourselves and the profession we love. *The Right Way of Death* is such a book and is an absolute must-read for anyone concerned about the nature and relevance of funeral service in our day."

—Daren B. Forbes, Vice President, West Region, Park Lawn Corporation

"Success in any business requires an obsessive focus on the customer—something many funeral homes understand in principle but forget in practice. *The Right Way of Death* not only tackles the problem, but offers insightful and practical advice in how to overcome it. If you work in the death care profession, read this book."

—Hamilton Jones, President,
Miller-Jones Mortuary & Crematory, California

"If a business book doesn't result in fear, anger, or excitement, then reading it is of little value. Eric Layer goes three for three. *The Right Way of Death* is of exceptional value to those willing to open their minds."

—Glenn Taylor, Chairman, Glenn Funeral Home, Kentucky

"*The Right Way of Death* is a thought-provoking dive that should stop any funeral home owner, manager, or front-line staff member in their tracks. Eric's book will push you to innovate, take risks, and challenge the industry norms."

—Scott Newton, President, Graystone Associates, Inc.

"Mr. Layer's book will truly stir emotions for the funeral industry. On almost all points he has identified the issues, most of them longstanding, that today's funeral profession faces. He does it in a way that is easily understandable, and will promote deep reflection and curiosity for the funeral director who chooses to read the book. I, for one, look forward to using Layer's thoughts to strengthen and improve our company. We should all thank him for taking the time and effort to get us to change positively in order to help those who need our help, expertise, and advice."

—Randy Schoedinger, CEO,
Schoedinger Funeral and Cremation Service, Ohio

"Nearly every day, we in funeral service must watch helplessly as families make decisions that we know might hinder their grief process. *The Right Way of Death* brings that pain into the open and carefully offers opportunities for funeral homes to realign with the families we serve—not through retreat, but by actively leaning into the truths of our calling."

—Bill McReavy, President,
Washburn-McReavy Funeral Chapels, Minnesota

"The way we see ourselves in funeral service is becoming entirely different from how the public sees us. *The Right Way of Death* will open your eyes and give you confidence to move forward and seize opportunity."

—Bill Chapman, Owner,
Chapman, Cole & Gleason Funeral Homes, Massachusetts

"*The Right Way of Death* is jam-packed with the truths at the core of the funeral business that are all too often forgotten. If you care about the future of the calling, this book will leave you challenged and invigorated. There is hard work to be done, but Layer provides the inspiration and motivation to do it.»

—Jake Johnson, President and CEO, Johnson Consulting Group

"*The Right Way of Death* is an outstanding read for anyone with curiosity regarding death, a topic of interest that is not often discussed. I have heard the quote, 'A compelling why will create a meaningful how.' Eric eloquently presents both the why and the how, as well as the ever-changing care of our loved ones after death. This book is a fascinating read for industry professionals and the general public. You will be glad you read it."

—Spencer M. Larkin, Vice President, Larkin Mortuary, Utah

THE RIGHT WAY OF DEATH

Restoring the American Funeral Business
to Its True Calling

ERIC LAYER

MPATH
PUBLISHING

mpathpublishing.com

To Alan Wood

Thank you for helping us do it right in 2004.

The Right Way of Death
Restoring the American Funeral Business to Its True Calling
Copyright © 2020 by Eric Layer. All Rights Reserved.

For more information about this title or to order other books and/or electronic media, contact the publisher:

M Path Publishing
Albuquerque, NM
mpathpublishing.com

ISBN:
978-1-7356109-2-4 (hardcover)
978-1-7356109-0-0 (paperback)
978-1-7356109-1-7 (ebook)

Printed in the United States of America

Interior design: Darlene Swanson • Van-garde Imagery

Table of Contents

Acknowledgments

"What is so delicious as a just and firm encounter of two, in a thought, in a feeling?"

—Ralph Waldo Emerson

A book is one of those special undertakings (like a backyard renovation) that exposes one's utter dependence on others. C.S. Lewis wrote, "I have no duty to be anyone's friend and no man in the world has a duty to be mine." In writing, I learn just how much I am indebted to others who had no obligation to offer me their friendship, support, encouragement, and insight, and yet who did so nonetheless. My name is on the cover, but I owe a debt of gratitude to so many others for what they've contributed to every single page.

First and foremost, to my parents, Paul and Corrie Layer, for their wisdom, instruction, and leadership. On the very most practical level, it was their teaching and willingness to educate a curious boy about their profession that provided the industry knowledge that constitutes the foundation of this book. But much more importantly, their example and prayerful guidance taught me about all the principles most important in life and death. Nothing I've learned since I left their house has been novel; it has only built on the foundation they laid.

To my business partners, Jonathan Lewis and David Ortega, who have taught me so much about how to do great work, but also about how to be good. Both of you are friends and brothers, and to strive together is a joy. To have a colleague who can contend with you in either heart or mind is a rare blessing. I have two who do both.

To our founder and my editor, Steve McKee, whose work I have stolen on almost every page. Steve has taught innumerable marketers and leaders how to think, and he is the giant upon whose shoulders we stand. And as if that wasn't enough, his command of the English language is such that his suggestions have improved my every paragraph.

To the book team: Shannon, I'm grateful for your unflappable support, kind spirit, and extensive research. Mat, you are the very paragon of an editor. The sharpness of your brain has honed my own work in both thought and diction, but the graciousness of your heart makes you a special joy to work with. I hope to have the opportunity to do so for many more years. Elizabeth, you've been improving my work since my very first day in this business; it's fitting that you would do so again here. Thank you for always finding a way to make it happen. Cassie and Marie, y'all are miracle workers, and I'm still astounded at what you pulled off (including plenty I'm sure I'll never know about) to make this book a reality. Cassie, I'm thankful for your loyal commitment to what we stand for, and for the wit you bring to every moment. Marie, I'm grateful for your friendship and for your dedication to our team. And Kim, dear and oldest friend: your support on this project has not only improved it, but has improved me, yet again, through your friendship and insight.

To the entire team at MW+C: I could not have written a single chapter had you not stepped up the way you heroically have. Thank you. Ana, for your determination and grit, especially in the face of loss. You have done it *right*. Kyle, for your teachability and resilience amidst a bizarre year. Pat, for ruthlessly making us all better. Dayna, for your grace and bedrock reliability, especially during chaos. Max, for never quitting until the job is done, and for always making sure we are equipped for whatever adventure we dream up. Craig, for just jumping in and blessing us all when you did. Jazmin, for spreadsheets and music. Stephanie, for keeping us all on the ball. Al, for your speed. Jymi, for your smiles. Jessica, for your enthusiasm.

And Maria. You've been writing our voice in this space since long before I ever showed up, and you've captured in a line what takes me a chapter. Your excitement about this stuff never ceases to make me smile, and the thought of handing you a copy was no small incentive to write this.

To the guys: Wade, Nathan, Sean, and Miles, for many fishing and hunting trips' worth of friendship, support, encouragement, wisdom, and brotherly love.

To so many in the business who made strong and early impressions through their commitment to service and selfless encouragement to mourning families. This book is both to you and from you in so many ways. As a young man, you gave me a model to follow of what it meant to be a gentleman and a leader. And in my career, you have offered me the opportunity to teach, but have invariably ended up teaching me: Chet, Bob, and Rick Stewart, Tom Antram, Duffy Swan, Karl Saltzman, Alan Wood, Daren Forbes, Michael Wellensiek, Dan Frakes, John Horan, Kevin Bean, Bill Chapman, John Blute, Hamilton Jones, Mike Kirikos, and so many others. Thank you for opening your doors to me, and thank you for the decades you've spent choosing to help families do the right thing at the worst time.

To my boys: coming home each day is a far greater joy than I ever could have asked for. "Dad" will always be my favorite job title. James, never lose your enthusiasm and earnestness. And Andrew, may your tender kindness always bring others the happiness that it does now. I hope you are both able to raise your families in a world that has figured out how to do a better job of saying goodbye, and that has to do so less frequently.

And finally, to my beautiful wife, Shannon, who is always my biggest fan and whose unyielding support comes in the form of tireless, relentless self-sacrifice for others. Your labor for our family and friends is to the glory of our God, the betterment of our sons, and the honor of our family's name. You, my dear, are my hero. Here's hail! to the rest of the road.

Thank you all.

A Note on Terminology

"Funeral service is not an industry. It's a calling."

I've heard this statement in some form hundreds of times in my life, and I completely, unequivocally agree with 50 percent of it.

Funeral service is absolutely a calling. The profession is one that forces its practitioners to face mortality (and all its grisly consequences) in the most intimate proximity, day in and day out. On its very best day, it requires service and empathy to people at their very worst. It requires long hours, public derision, and perhaps the toughest aspects of both blue-collar and white-collar work. It demands patience, grit, emotional health, organization, scientific aptitude, unyielding devotion to principles, literacy in a litany of world religions, and almost superhuman flexibility and compassion. And for that, it offers little gratitude and even less pay. You could argue that if you took the most demanding features of every job and put them all together, you would have the job description for a mortuary owner.

However, in my writing, I often refer to the American funeral business collectively as an industry. This is primarily because our language offers me no alternative. Funeral homes are businesses. I am a business consultant. I have written about the collective future of those businesses, as a whole. In the English language, "industry" is the best and most expedient way of referencing such a category. Not only is this often the best word available, there is no lexical reason why it is incorrect.

But the more important reason is this: in no way are "industry" and "calling" mutually exclusive terms. In fact, quite the opposite. A calling is very often achieved *most* effectively when it coincides with economic interest. Organizations and employees who stand to profit more when they serve more effectively are simply more likely to be effective. Nonprofits and government agencies certainly employ individuals called to their work, but in the absence of the motivation of profits, they sometimes achieve their aims less efficiently, with less innovation, and with less longevity than their industrial counterparts. If funeral service is indeed a calling, then it should seek the most efficacious means of delivering the object of that calling.

From pharmaceuticals to manufacturing to agriculture to technology, the greatest improvements in history, that have done the most to ease the burden upon humanity, have been industrial in nature. Funeral directors have been shamed and scolded for the fact that profit is gained from the services offered, but this is wrong. You *should* profit from them, because you take on risk and sacrifice your time to provide value for which people are willing to pay. And the value you provide is very great indeed.

It is impossible to argue that anything generating $20 billion per year is not an industry. But again, the fact that it does is not something of which to be ashamed, especially if funeral professionals seek to elevate the work of their industry by treating it as a calling. The very purpose of my work, in fact, is to restore the heart and mindset of calling to the industry. I believe that this can only be done by understanding the industrial forces acting upon it. In funeral service, as in other industries, economic successes and failures are invaluable clues as to how to fine-tune the business to better serve the aims and purposes of the calling.

I am convinced, through my firm's quarter-century of work with, and research of, virtually every industry and type of business, that those firms which do the best job of operating missionally and fulfilling their calling are also those with the best understanding of their business, and those which most unapologetically work as a business. There are plenty of companies that succeed at business but fail to work as a calling. But there are no companies that fail at business and still are able to deliver on the promise of their calling.

So, if you believe (as I do) that funeral service is a calling, you are exactly the person for whom I have written this book. There are not many of you left, so I am thankful that you have found your way here. I hope you will forgive me for referring to your work collectively as an industry, and that you will perhaps give me the chance to articulate why a better understanding of your industry is crucial to the future of your calling.

Because it is a calling that must be protected and allowed to continue.

Introduction

I've been writing this book for thirty years.

Over the course of his career, my father was a funeral director, embalmer, cemetery president, death care entrepreneur, and mortuary owner. He held both a general contractor's license and a funeral director's license so that he could oversee the construction of new mortuaries and mausoleums as business expanded (in the '80s and '90s, business was expanding). My mother spent more than a decade in funeral service herself—she and my father met when he was head embalmer and she was a secretary at French Mortuary in Albuquerque. They were married the next year in the chapel of the mortuary he built, where she would return to work as front office supervisor decades later. For me, it was an idyllic way to grow up, and a comforting picture of the normalcy of death. Like thousands of other children (many of today's mortuary owners) raised around family funeral homes in America, it never occurred to me that there was anything unusual about life in a mortuary.

During my childhood, even our holidays revolved around death. At Christmastime, our mantel was adorned with bronze "Twelve Days of Christmas" ornaments—annual gifts from the Matthews Bronze (headstone) Company. As a first grader, I was responsible for educating the local Scout troop on how to properly differentiate between civilian and military headstones, so they knew which would be marked with a tiny American flag on Memorial Day. The memorial-park-style cemetery was a ten-year-old's dream, and my childhood memories involved excavators in the back lot and bike rides through acres of tree-lined (and grave-lined) roads. At one point in my teens, when I was considering a career in medicine, I joined my father in the prep room to watch him work, learning about anatomy and life and grief all at once.

And when death occurred, whether in our own family or our circle of friends, there was always a cadre of supporters from the office and a meticulously crafted set of rituals to shepherd us all through. From a young age, I understood that the funeral is for the family and not for the deceased, that seeing the body is a painful but necessary component of confronting death, and that you'll never regret going to the funeral. Some might call it indoctrination, but just like the Layers were Baptists and Bills fans, there were things we believed because Dad was a funeral director.

I distinctly remember those evenings when my father was on call (long after he should have been, given his seniority, but to be a funeral director is to be all things at all times) and a "first call" would come late at night. The voice with which he would express both empathy and a reassuring command of the process was one I recognize to this day, and one that I've heard many of my clients use since—almost as if there is a tone of voice innate to the profession. It filled me with pride to think that at another family's worst moment, my family would be there.

I remember even more distinctly the subtle (and sometimes not-so-subtle) frustration that so often marked our family's dinner table conversations. I remember the indignation I felt as a young boy when my mother explained to me that a particularly vocal acquaintance believed that funeral homes took advantage of the bereaved. I remember the disappointment when this friend or that chose direct cremation, especially for a loved one whom we wished to mourn ourselves. And I remember elementary school playground conversations, precociously trying to educate my peers on the merits of burial over cremation.

Since then, I've observed in other "funeral families" the same powerful need to evangelize for the family business. "If people only knew what we know..." Society has developed its own opinions and perspectives on death, and these are often at odds with the conclusions developed by the people most acquainted with end-of-life preparations. It's not surprising that this is frustrating for my family or yours. That frustration stems not from self-righteousness or greed on the part of funeral directors. Just like any expert, it is impossible for a funeral director to spend decades caring for people and watching them mourn without coming to some conclusions about what works best. And it is equally impossible for any caring individual to see firsthand the results of both good and bad decisions and not attempt to share that knowledge with others—especially when in constant contact with the people who need that perspective the most. It's a tragedy, then, when these attempts to help are viewed not with gratitude, but with derision and suspicion.

Most professions dispense advice gained through experience without suffering any such contempt. Some, like mechanics, are similarly mistrusted. But the stakes of a poorly done car repair are so much lower than those of a poorly done grief process. You can always take your Volvo back into the shop; a lack of closure over a loved one can cause a lifetime of pain. And so funeral directors find themselves in an impossible Catch-22. They are the people most capable of helping the public at a particular moment of need, and perhaps the least trusted to do so. They're expected at once to guide and to be silent; to be trustworthy and to live with being distrusted; to enter moments of great vulnerability with empathy and yet never overstep.

It's a hard job. And it's grown harder over the years. Funeral homes are no longer expanding like they were for my father in the '80s. Books have been published to discredit the profession. Laws have been passed to regulate it. Products and cottage industries have popped up claiming to provide alternatives to it. It seems ever more impossible to plan for an ever more ambiguous future.

Perhaps in response, everybody is looking for the next big thing. You can plant your loved one with a tree. You can shoot her into space. You can make him into jewelry. You can strip pews out of chapels, and build reception centers, and tack on "cremations" and "celebrations of life" after "funerals" in your name. You can liquefy a body through alkaline hydrolysis. You can bury a body in an eco-friendly casket. You can buy caskets at Costco. You can let a family see Grandma for the last time in a slumber bed. No doubt you've chuckled, rolled your eyes, invested, and considered your way through a list fifty times this long of new products, offerings, and concepts claiming to rethink the industry. It seems somebody invents a new death care product every day (some of them unfit to print).

But none of these have solved the business problem—they have simply added on to it, eager to get their share of the pie without offering a substantial opportunity to grow it. The foundation continues to sag, now under the weight of new burdens that only continue to multiply. The dilemmas facing funeral directors only complexify with each new product rolled out. There are now more products to showcase, more models to compete against, and more offerings that families have inexplicably learned to ask for.

All the while, funeral directors are caught up in the "split personality of the calling."[1] They must be, as I've been reminded in mortuaries from coast to coast, "all things to all people." People expect them to be efficient and empathetic, professional but human, willing to "get their hand slapped" but quick to withdraw when they do, counselor and salesperson, confidant and stranger. And, most importantly, they are expected to be both leaders and followers. They are required to provide guidance and direction during the most confusing and disorienting experience life can throw at us, but they are also reminded daily that they're not trusted to lead, not qualified to counsel, and not equipped to guide.

The family, too, is caught in an impossible position. They have been told since the '60s not to trust funeral directors (for that matter, they've been told since the '60s not to trust any institutions). And yet, they find themselves less experientially equipped to deal with death than any prior generation. John Horan of Horan & McConaty in Denver shared with me the remarkable insight that many people in their 60's have never experienced a loss within their inner circle. Thanks to unprecedented medical advancements, you can be into your 60s without having buried a parent, or perhaps even without having ever attended a funeral. Harder times with shorter life expectancies better prepared people for death. Funerals were common societal events. One had a lifetime of practice to learn how to grieve. But today, it is easier to avoid death for most of life, and funerals have become a novelty: unfamiliar, unpleasant, and uncanny.

To reconnect with this new customer in this new context will unequivocally require change. This is the greatest challenge. It's not the funeral directors' fault that they've been so resistant to change; death itself is unchanging. Even farmers have seen revolutionary improvements in the way food is produced, but dead bodies and grieving people, for all intents and purposes, are just the same as they were when the Egyptians were embalming in the shadows of the newly constructed pyramids. If the subject matter hasn't evolved, why should the business? This work is steeped in tradition, religion, and permanence. It is no wonder that a company with crucifixes, menorahs, and pulpits stashed behind its chapel would be hesitant to reinvent every five years like a Silicon Valley startup.

In fact, tech companies reinvent not because they are inherently more innovative, but because they're forced to. If Google doesn't stay sharp today, somebody else will be on its heels tomorrow. With no such rapid development spurring the funeral business on, there's little incentive to evolve—and no immediacy. While some of the funeral directors I meet with do fit the stereotype (stodgy, conservative, unyielding to progress), most do not. In fact, I find that most funeral directors desperately want to change; they just don't know exactly what to change *to*. Here, tech might have the easier road. Customers want more data, more convenience, more speed. But what do funeral customers want? It is probably fair to say that even they don't know. So, a funeral director's obstacle isn't so much tradition and conservatism as it is overcoming ambiguity. This might be one reason funeral homes (like hospitals and financial institutions) often work so hard on process improvement. Since it is unclear, or even illegal, to invent, they feel that all they can do is optimize.

But that optimization is part of the problem. As they get better and better at hitting target numbers, perfecting sales tactics, or setting up the right preneed machine, they make it more difficult to step away from those finely-tuned engines when needed. People like certainty. Apart from CPAs, funeral directors may be predisposed to prefer certainty more than anyone—what is more guaranteed than death and taxes? As certainty and expertise grow around a particular product, practice, or process, and as the future and its opportunities appear ever more ambiguous, the industry is ever more hesitant to stray from the safety of numbers and data. It is much more reassuring to look at an employee's year-over-year numbers than it is to look in the mirror and ask whether we have the right business model anymore. One feels like adjusting the cruise control. The other feels like throwing the steering wheel out the window.

An example of dangerously stacking the deck against change is when funeral directors tell themselves, "We'll always have the body." I've heard this line at boardroom tables and industry conference stages—a claim meant to reassure a sputtering trade that the death business is still as sure a bet as it ever was. But it's a shaky foundation on which to build your business. Countless trends within death care, and even more case studies from other trades, all point to the same frightening truths: nothing is constant, and businesses (and industries) that rest on their laurels are the most vulnerable to new competition.

There are other lies that funeral service has bought into. For example, the industry's fixed pool of demand has led to a widespread conviction among funeral directors that they must be "all things to all people." The thought of losing even one family to a competitor is paralyzing when you are hardwired with a scarcity mindset. You cannot increase demand—nor would you want to. All you can do is squabble for the demand that already exists, resulting in a limited, cutthroat market and a startling willingness to compromise. But the consequences of this mindset are far more insidious than funeral homes recognize. It results in not only a feeble, unfocused brand image, but limited power to credibly serve families when they walk through the door. Funeral directors have suffered mightily from the conviction that they must be jacks of all trades, rarely recognizing the painful truth that they are perceived as masters of none.

Perhaps the most dangerous lie of them all is about merchandise. It's been said many ways: "Families like the merchandise." "This product is selling really well." Or perhaps worst of all, "We need product sales to keep us in business." Merchandise has its place, but funeral homes should be aware of the dangers of becoming hooked on this particular drug. When you usher a family into a casket selection room, you stop being a counselor and start being a salesman. It doesn't matter whether your associates make a commission or not. It doesn't matter if your prices are the lowest in town. When you're selling merchandise, you are confirming their worst assumptions about the industry—and they're bringing some pretty negative assumptions to the table to begin with.

It's not your fault. None of this is. Funeral service is a strange beast; it's a business created to meet end-of-life societal obligations that has been poked and prodded and harassed into providing this or doing that as those societal obligations have changed again and again and again. Laws meant to keep you accountable have only made the process more awkward and have made innovation more difficult. Hollywood productions and sensationalized news have planted bizarre fears and expectations in the minds of the families you try to serve. Everything from the economy to religion to politics to entertainment seems to have taken its pound of flesh, until there's little left. You are simply not running the business you want to run.

Despite all the challenges and misperceptions, however, the most important news is this: you have been right all along. Funeral directors have a belief deep in their souls that they struggle to articulate. But you should articulate it, and loudly, because it's true. It's probably the reason you got into the business. It likely drives your work each day. It's likely integrated in your training and sales processes, your mission statement, the "about us" page of your website, and even your GPL. But it's also an idea you've been told as a professional, for decades, that is wrong to give voice to. It's an idea that sounds offensive. It's an idea that's often misunderstood, even though most families intuitively believe it as well. It's a truth that needs to be exhumed and resurrected, because it's the truth that is foundational to your business. And it is the only thing that will save it.

There is a right way to do this.

There is a right way to grieve. There is a right way to "do" death. There is a right way to approach a loss. There are practices, steps, actions, decisions, and yes, even purchases, that will result in an easier, more complete farewell to the one lost. Avoiding these steps brings pain and guilt and confusion and expense in measures that are tragically unnecessary. Following them brings healing, comfort, and reassurance.

And nobody is better equipped, better positioned, or more knowledgeable in how to guide a family through that "right way" than you.

Not that long ago, morticians shared a sacred place in the community alongside pastors and community leaders. They were trusted to guide families through a painful time when they needed guidance the most. They were revered and able to command the price they asked because the work they did was perceived as highly valuable. Ironically, in a time when families have become more lost and less experienced with death, a time that has seen a decline in our exposure to both pastors and community leaders, people have become more hesitant to turn to funeral directors, even as they need them more.

It is my hope to help morticians rediscover their souls—that they brush off the dirt and rust that has obscured their former glory and restore the public's perception of their office to one of leadership, confidence, and hope for their communities. The work required to do so will be slow and hard. It will require a grief of its own, laying to rest much of what the profession has become. But those who are called to do it are those who have chosen one of the most challenging, emotionally demanding, and laborious vocations of our time. America's funeral directors and funeral home owners are up to the task.

Funeral service is a noble profession. It can be saved. And more importantly, it is well worth saving.

Section 1: You've Been Right All Along

Chapter 1
The Split Personality of the Calling

1963 was a rough year for funeral service.

Caitlin Doughty, the famous crematory-operator-turned-author, called it "cremation's year."[1] In July, the Catholic Church lifted its historical ban on cremation. The same year, the Funeral Consumers Alliance was founded, its stated goal to "keep tabs on the prices and practices of the funeral industry."[2]

And it was in January of 1963 that *The American Way of Death* was published—Jessica Mitford's meticulously researched, ruthlessly worded, virulent attack on funeral service. In her book, Mitford railed against everything from product sales to morticians as grief counselors. She blasted pricing tactics, bemoaned the structure of the industry, and took aim at the most sacred institutions of funeral service. Hardly a stone was left unturned, and there was scarcely a component of the funeral director's work with which Mitford did not take issue.

The FTC's Funeral Rule was enacted two decades later, and in her 1996 updated revision, Mitford all but accepted responsibility for the sweeping legislation that redefined funeral service as we know it and put every mortuary in America on a short leash. She may well have been right to take credit. Directly or indirectly, her book gave America its perspective on, and suspicion of, funeral service. Mitford did for Americans planning funerals what Upton Sinclair did for Americans eating bologna.

For all her research and conviction, it's tough to tell what Jessica

Mitford intended as the result of her work. Her frustration with funeral service was clear; less so was her objective. To reform the business? To end it? The only calls to action Mitford offers are methods for consumers to avoid or outmaneuver funeral professionals; she never offers a roadmap for professionals to reform their trade.

Whatever her intent, the result has certainly been destruction. The industry has not been reformed. In many ways, it has been cornered into doubling down on Mitford's original complaints. Weighed down by the Funeral Rule, bad press, and an ugly consumer suspicion of practitioners, funeral service seems mired in personal shame and unable to pull itself out of the pit. Funeral care in America may be more heavily regulated, more deeply distrusted, and less lucrative than it was in 1963, but it is by no means better equipped to serve the public. Ironically, many of Mitford's sharpest critiques (merchandise revenue, sales techniques) are ostensibly the only ways for the modern funeral home to survive amidst the uncertainty and pressure wrought by her work. Even today, the online reviews of *The American Way of Death* read like a complaint forum against the local mortuary. Everybody, it would seem, has a bone to pick and a story to tell.

While Mitford was never sympathetic to funeral directors, she did unwittingly describe one of the most daunting challenges facing them. Funeral professionals, Mitford wrote, would "vastly prefer to be looked upon as 'trained professionals with high standards of ethical conduct,' but the exigencies of their trade still force them into the role of 'merchants of a rather grubby order.'"[3] Mitford concludes that funeral service is marked by "...the split personality of the calling, arising out of its inherent contradictions."[4]

While her description is by no means flattering, it raises an important question: what exactly should funeral directors be? Are they akin to waiters, with a responsibility to deliver exactly what a family asks but never suggest anything else? Or are they leaders, duty-bound to guide a family toward the decisions that will serve them best? Do they exist only for the deceased, to quietly handle the body and its disposition? Or is the surviving family's health and well-being something with which they should concern themselves? Are they counselors with a role of providing compassionate guidance? Or salespeople with numbers to hit? Should they be empathetic to reflect the family's state of mind? Or stoic, true to the fact that they have done this a thousand times? Should they act like the trustworthy servants they are? Or should they acknowledge that they know they're perceived as self-interested and untrustworthy?

Every time they answer "both," America's morticians find their mission increasingly diluted and obscured. They must train their employees to handle a confusing and daunting list of paradoxes, and their customers expect them to impossibly become all of the above. What Mitford called "the split personality of the calling"[5] has led to the paralysis of funeral directors since even before her book hit shelves. Funeral directors live in a precarious situation. Mitford, of all people, seemed to recognize this, even while she was disparaging them. The role of being simultaneously guardian and salesperson, leader and attendant, confidant and business owner—it's a terribly thin line to walk. All funeral directors know it; they can hardly introduce themselves or answer the friendly question of, "What do you do?" without being put on the defensive. They are instantly associated with someone's worst experience of death and subjected to a stern lecture on the worst assumptions about the business. What are they to do?

All of this has led me, over the last few years, to ask a question of funeral directors and funeral home owners every time I get the chance. It started as a way to get a particular client on the record, but when the response was the opposite of what I expected, it grew into a sort of national experiment. My data is purely anecdotal, but the question—and how you answer it—betrays an important understanding about modern funeral service.

"Is there a right way to grieve?"

If the answer is yes, that has implications for your business. Certain products, approaches, and even customers are "righter" than others, and your work is infused with a moral imperative to support them. Doctors, builders, mechanics—those professions in which there is a "right way" to do things—are duty-bound to do it right, and to provide for their customers a degree of consultative expertise. If there is a right way, then a funeral director is hired not just to get the job done, but to do it right, and to make recommendations to help the family do the same.

If the answer is no, that too has implications. The job must simply get done, and there's no objectivity beyond what the customer wants. Retailers and restaurants come to mind here. The customer shows up when they want something, and it's essentially the duty of the provider to give them what they ask for. In all but the finest restaurants, it doesn't matter if the chef believes potatoes would pair perfectly with that dish; if the customer wishes to substitute a side salad, then that's what they must receive. In food service and retail, the customer is always right. Conversely, in medicine and engineering, that concept is laughable; the expert is hired precisely because of the customer's lack of expertise. So, we must ask into which category funeral service falls. Is there a right way to do this? Or are we simply retailers who serve at the pleasure of the customer?

Mitford's book—and in many ways, her life's work—was built on the premise that there is no "right" way to do death. She contended that funeral service had duped the public into believing there is solely as a means to swindle them out of money. The families you serve, and arguably our culture at large, has swallowed this perspective hook, line, and sinker. When she died in 1996, Mitford's husband had her cremated for $475. No funeral, no family present, no celebration or recognition of any kind.[6] Just a direct cremation. Mitford was dead set on debunking the notions that morticians are experts in grief and that there are psychological benefits to a funeral or viewing. If she was right, that has important implications for how you should do business. It would mean you need to focus on whatever is going to sell the most products or meet demand the most expediently. It would mean you should build your company around the product *du jour*. If jewelry is in, then jewelry should be stocked on the walls. If the market wants direct cremation, then you should close up shop on the full-service side. It's a clean, straightforward approach—and one to which many of your competitors (including some very well-funded ones) are unapologetically committed.

On the other hand, if Mitford was wrong, and if there really is a right way to handle death, that has implications too. For one, it would mean that the ever-less-popular traditions against which Mitford railed so sharply really do have value, and that mortuaries were never wrong to promote them. It would also mean that a mortician's work is not simply to deliver what clients *want*, but to work toward providing what they *need*. This is a more complicated road, but it's arguably a more fulfilling one, and even a more lucrative one. It's said, apocryphally but nonetheless poignantly, that Henry Ford was suspicious of design by focus group: "If I had asked people what they wanted, they would have said faster horses."[7] If you're looking for innovation—and success—the place to start probably isn't a customer satisfaction survey.

No, if there's a right way to do this, it means looking to something higher than the whims of public tastes. Most of us intuitively understand that a business has to be grounded in something with more staying power than what will move product this month. This is the very definition of a mission. No doubt you have a mission statement of your own in your office or on your website somewhere. But there's a difference between having a mission statement and working missionally. A mission is not a product or a model or an approach. Your mission is what you exist to do. Your reason for being. A moral imperative. In the last century, this shouldn't have changed, and in another century, it will still be the same. Great companies have great missions, and they set a permanent foundation upon which to build.

In January of 1977, Steve Jobs and Steve Wozniak wrote down the mission statement of Apple Computer Inc. "Apple is dedicated to the empowerment of man—to making personal computing accessible to each and every individual so as to help change the way we think, work, learn, and communicate."[8]

The statement reads as remarkably prescient. It's hard to imagine that Jobs and Wozniak really understood just how much would be achieved by their company to this end over the next four decades. But that's exactly what a mission statement should be: unbounded by a particular time or situation. In 1977, Jobs and Wozniak had a specific idea in mind of what individually accessible personal computing meant—and in 1977, it involved computers the size of dressers. By the '90s, that had evolved into something very different. In 2001, it meant the iPod, and by 2007, the iPhone. The company that was building computers in 1977 was by the early 2000s a service company with only a fraction of its revenue coming from computer sales. More than half of Apple's margins in 2020 came from storage services, app subscriptions, licensing, and warranties—platforms that didn't even exist in 1977.

If Jobs and Wozniak's mission statement had been "to sell personal computers," Apple would be a very different company today. Instead, they looked beyond their business model, upward at an idea that transcended what they could have imagined at the time. In the same way, your mission shouldn't be tied to any assumptions about how you'll work, what you'll sell, or how you'll make money.

When you think about your mission, don't become distracted by that gold-framed mission *statement* hanging on your wall. Usually those are simply an exercise in wordsmithing, a fixation of a board of directors 20 years ago that employees don't remember and that management doesn't apply. Instead, think about the mission itself. Why do you get out of bed in the morning? What would be lost to your community, besides your revenue stream and a few jobs, if you closed up for good? What would be different if your next owner were a big conglomerate instead of your son or daughter, or your hand-picked successor? Chances are you have some strong feelings about those questions, and chances are those are clues to your mission.

Your *model*, on the other hand, is something completely different. Your model is the *means* by which you are working toward that mission. The model will change. In fact, the model must never stop changing. Apple's model was product sales in 1977, service revenues in 2020, and will be something else entirely in 2070.

The trick is understanding the difference between mission and model. And as my firm has researched hundreds of private mortuaries around the country, I've become convinced that almost nobody in the business truly understands that distinction. Shockingly, less than half of mortuary owners nationwide agree with the statement that they need a new business model.[9] This is a shocking, indefensible position, because *every* business needs a new business model. And death care's current model is a century old, rooted in societal norms and structures that no longer exist. Almost everything your children buy works differently than it did a decade ago. Don't expect them to plan your funeral the same way your grandfather planned his father's.

It doesn't end there. An incredible 71 percent of funeral home owners believe that their customers fully understand the value they provide. If that was true, direct cremation wouldn't be on the rise, Jessica Mitford's book wouldn't have been a bestseller, and Silicon Valley wouldn't be investing millions to provide an alternative.[10] Four out of five funeral home owners believe they embrace change—again, a shocking figure considering how little the way they do business has really changed, even amidst rapidly evolving customer expectations.[11] The ubiquitous belief in this industry is that it will be able to do things the way it always has, ad infinitum.

In other words, funeral service is treating its model like its mission. It's no wonder why. So little has changed in the model over the past century that the products and services have become synonymous with the needs they meet. And the two are confused. The industry talks a great deal about percentages of direct cremation while thinking relatively little about how many families were actually helped to confront their loss. Many owners can tell you what sales did month over month but have no idea whether Mrs. Smith went back to visit her husband's grave on Memorial Day. And they know that Legacy Touch trinkets sell like hotcakes, but they aren't really sure whether they are actually cherished as the treasured memorials as which they're sold.

Confusing model and mission is a twofold danger for this business. First, funeral service has grown foggy regarding that for which it really exists. The lack of clarity regarding its mission is not entirely the industry's fault, but it is certainly a problem. The mission (again, not the framed placard on the wall but the actual idea we communicate) of most funeral homes today is a thick, cloudy gumbo: a good helping of tradition, some salesmanship and business best-practice, a wistful remembrance of the golden years three decades ago, a fuzzy reading of futurism and social commentary, and a heaping dose of fear—fear of family's displeasure, of bankruptcy, of lawsuits, and of an FTC inspector with an obscure reading of the Funeral Rule.

One branch manager I interviewed told a story about a grumpy old cynic who came in to make arrangements for his wife. It was clear to my client that the gentleman was in denial over his loss, and despite the funeral director's best efforts, he wasn't budging. Direct cremation, no funeral. At length, the funeral director discussed the psychological ramifications of not having a chance to say goodbye, the power of a viewing, and the importance of a ceremony for the deceased's grandchildren, if not for the gentleman himself. Still, nothing. Just as the skeptic was leaving, he noticed a few pieces of thumbprint jewelry on the merchandise display, and agreed to buy a few for his granddaughters. The funeral director was ready to high-five me for "a breakthrough."

I hated to be cynical, but I couldn't help but be confused by his elation. The man was still avoiding a funeral for his wife, and it seemed doubtful that a few baubles were going to change his denial. But such is the position of an industry on the ropes. With so many different and even conflicting missions (don't upset the family, don't let us go out of business, don't let them do a direct cremation, don't let them walk across the street) and an impossible situation to navigate, we sometimes celebrate for even the most minimal (and opposing) reasons. This is the world of missionlessness. We're unsure what exactly we're aiming for, so we take whatever we can get.

The other side of that double-edged sword is just as sharp. If we conflate mission and model, we will die on meaningless hills, unwilling to change because we assign to models and tactics and tools the value that should be reserved for a higher purpose.

I once met with another highly regarded funeral director who shared with me that he felt the firm absolutely needed to evolve, but never at the expense of fundamentals. Wanting to clarify, I asked, "What are the fundamentals?"

"Wearing black suits," he responded with deadpan earnestness. "And caskets, and limousines, and holding doors open for families."

His answer stunned me, because it betrayed the same foundational misunderstanding that I have since found is common in the industry. Whether it's time to give up on black suits, limousines, and caskets is a valid question about which competent businesspeople can disagree. It might be time to let these things go in Phoenix, while they'll still be profitable for decades in rural Kentucky. But there is simply no room for disagreement on this: *these things are absolutely not fundamentals.* They are executions. Applications. Tools. They may or may not get you closer to the essential mission toward which you work. To confuse them with the mission itself is a fatal error because you'll then protect to the death things that simply aren't worth protecting. If a new product, or a different approach, allows you to accomplish the mission just as well, then let's move on. Refusing to change your mission is worth going out of business over, but refusing to change your model will *put* you out of business.

History is replete with companies which have mistaken the difference. Radio Shack enshrined with mission-like permanence its model of a cookie-cutter store size and format and refused to evolve when big-box stores, and then online retailers, attacked its space. Borders was so naively committed to its brick-and-mortar model that it handed Amazon the keys to its kingdom, not even recognizing the internet bookseller as a competitor. (Amazon, on the other hand, recognized shrewdly that the two companies had the same mission—selling books—but that Amazon had a far superior model by which to do so.) Within the quickly evolving world of fast-casual and home-delivery food service, fast food brands (whose drive-through model no longer quite delivers on their mission of convenient dining) have struggled to keep up.

Caskets. Viewings. Rosaries. Openings and closings. Graves. Niches. Urns. Limos. Hearses. Removals. Embalmings. Cremations. GPLs. Funerals. Celebrations of life. Chapels. Black suits. Ties. Lapel pins. Every single one of these is part of a model. An approach. A tool. An implement. Some of them are in high demand. Others are still the right way to do things. Others are downright outdated. (I won't tell you which is which; that's up to you.) The fact that something is part of a model doesn't mean that we must abandon it. It just means that we acknowledge it's subservient to a higher mission. It's *not* non-negotiable.

When we treat our model as non-negotiable, we become unwilling to change, which simply doesn't work. No industry in human history has ever been able to apply the same model for any considerable period of time without evolution. There is a 100 percent mortality rate for businesses who don't change their model. Sears was once synonymous with retail. Today it's history.

Consider this: If your mission was to provide heat to homes, one thousand years ago your model would have been selling firewood. A hundred years ago it would have been coal. Today, it's natural gas. Someday, it will be something else. But as the world changes, and technology changes, so must the model, because new and better means of achieving the mission constantly become available. You might have the sharpest axe in town, but as soon as your competition has a chainsaw, you must either change or die.

Back to my big question.

Every time I meet with funeral directors, I ask whether there is actually a right way to grieve. Usually I wait for a moment in the conversation when they're expressing frustration with social trends, or complaining that direct cremations are up, or arguing about whether deregulation in the industry is a good thing.

In other words, I wait for the moment when they're talking about families doing it wrong. I've asked the question from coast to coast, of dozens of different funeral directors, from tiny 100-case firms to nationally-recognized major players. *Is there a right way to do the process of death?*

To this day, no one has ever told me that there is.

Usually, there's palpable awkwardness as they try to answer diplomatically. A few will answer outright with a "no," or an "of course not." Some will furrow their brows and think deeply, as though they've never consciously contemplated this before. But one hundred percent of the time, the answer is in the negative. The tragedy is the timing. I'm sitting in a room full of competent, skilled professionals, with decades (if not centuries) of experience amongst them, who have just been discussing with detail and expertise all of the consequences of doing death *wrong*. And yet they're hamstrung, whether by guilt, political correctness, confusion, or something else, absolutely unable to admit that there is a way to do it *right*.

Obviously, it's the word "right" that holds people up. Nobody wants to appear too rigid, too audacious, or too prejudiced. We've strayed from saying that there is a right way to do anything – from parenting to religion to career paths. Inclusion, tolerance, and open-mindedness are the watchwords of our culture. We're taught in school that there are no stupid questions. A century ago, pounding your fist on the table and proclaiming a right way might have been expected; today it just feels rude and narrow-minded.

And yet...

There is a right way to conduct almost every professional process. If I'm going to have a cancer removed, I want my surgeon to believe firmly and confidently that his approach is the best way to do it. If I'm spending a few thousand dollars to have my transmission replaced, you better believe I want it done right. Even in more subjective practices, like interior design, marketing, or art, there are well-established norms for producing and critiquing good work. You would be hard-pressed to find a creative director or an architect or a museum curator who tolerates the notion of absolute subjectivity in their employees' work. There *is* bad art, bad design, and bad advertising, and those things result when the practitioner departs from the right, established, studied, true, and proven ways of plying one's craft.

It's vital to note that a "right way" does not imply rigidity and pre-scriptiveness. Within even a single school of architecture or design there are endless opportunities for innovation and creative expression. To say that the "right" way to do art is to carve marble statues in the Renaissance style would be ridiculous. But to extrapolate from that to say that there is no such thing as bad art would be equally ridiculous. I suspect that funeral directors have been so pigeonholed as rigid, cold, and unaccommodating that after decades of being browbeaten, they've thrown the baby out with the bathwater and are afraid and unclear about what constitutes right grief at all.

If there was a "split personality" in funeral service before Mitford wrote her book, then her efforts have only multiplied it. If it was confusing to be both a confidant and a salesman in 1963, try doing it in an era when both are considered out of bounds. It is nothing short of tragic that Mitford and other critics have hammered funeral service into its present deflated, confused state—not merely a split personality, but a shattered one.

There is a right way to do death. And there is a wrong way. Avoidance, nonconfrontation, fear of emotion, suppression—all of these are wrong and will result in a stunted grief process. You know this as a professional, you were taught it in mortuary college, and you have seen it borne out in experience. Confronting, communicating, gathering, memorializing, processing, reflecting—these are healthy. This isn't about picking one tradition or another, or one venue over another; you can do a funeral "right" in a place outside of a funeral home, and every culture on earth has rituals and norms in place to shepherd the bereaved through loss and back into routine.

Today we pretend that passively disposing of Mom without any ceremony is as valid a path as mourning her. We have accepted the ridiculous notion that someone who has never been to a funeral is equipped to decide for a person's entire extended community that the funeral isn't important. The comfort of the moment ("funerals are creepy") is inexplicably considered to bear equal weight to the health of the long-term ("I just wish I'd had a chance to say goodbye"). All of this is unprecedented in human history.

When COVID-19 or 9/11 deny us the opportunity to mourn together or with the body of our deceased, it is considered a tragedy, and tomes are written about grieving in such strange times. But when unintentionally harmful decisions on the part of a few uninformed family members deny that same opportunity to themselves and to others, not a word is said—and those who have the most valuable perspective and the greatest expertise find themselves under the most strongly-imposed gag order.

In "The Death of Expertise," Tom Nichols argues that the United States "is now a country obsessed with the worship of its own ignorance."[12] Nichols paints a sobering picture of a society crippled by the misguided view that the opinion of someone with ten minutes of online study is just as valid as the opinion of an expert with decades of experience. He tells a true story of a college sophomore arguing arrogantly with a revered astrophysicist. At one point, unable to convince the expert, the student shrugs and huffs, "Well, your guess is as good as mine." The astrophysicist wisely reminds him, "No, no, no. My guesses are much, *much* better than yours."[13]

Funeral directors are experts, and it is high time they said so. You cannot serve thousands, or tens of thousands, of grieving families without picking up some clues about what works and what doesn't. If you help a couple scatter their son's ashes twenty years after his death, and then hold them as they weep with relief after finally being able to say goodbye, you're not wrong to advise the next family you meet that they should reconsider taking their child's remains home with them. If you see the changed expression in a young man's face after he's able to sob over the open casket of his brother, you're more than entitled to tell the next family that a viewing might be the hardest thing they ever do, but it will be worth it. And if you watch from your office when a young widow returns to visit her husband's grave, you're not obligated to sit quietly by when the next family in your office says that memorials and places to visit aren't really important.

There is hardly a psychologist alive who has spent more time studying mourning families than the average American funeral home owner. Your profession is licensed, trained, and regulated. There are schools dedicated to teaching your craft, and you spend decades honing it. You likely have personal experience with death—either you grew up around the profession or had a close personal loss that you had to deal with yourself. All of this adds up to a trade that far surpasses the threshold of what constitutes expertise. And that itself constitutes an undeniable moral imperative. You do know what's going to help, and what isn't. You do know what is healthy and what's not. You do know which families are going to be okay, and which are going to struggle.

You have to be willing to say so.

The pressures against you here are immense, to be sure. Society has been conditioned to distrust you. Many of the industry's assumptions and approaches, as we will read, have solidified that distrust. Death care as a whole is confused over what to let go of and what to cling to. Funeral directors are like a baseball player in a slump, unsure about what to change and who to listen to, paralyzed by blow after blow to their confidence.

But the best way to get out of a slump is to acknowledge it and get back to the basics. The profession needs to do just that. To move forward, you must gather those fragmented pieces of the calling to rebuild a moral imperative for the industry. A true north to which people can look. The mission must again be made clear so that you can lead families, employees, and communities in the right direction. This is no small task, but it must be done. It must be done for the same reason your forebears founded your business, and likely for the reason you got into the business in the first place.

They need you.

Chapter 2
A Lost Generation

I once heard a funeral director tell a story of a woman who came in to make arrangements for her recently deceased husband. She was poorly dressed, a bit disheveled, and it was obvious she hadn't had a shower in days. Nonetheless, with every choice to be made she selected one of the most expensive options: a beautiful, high-end casket, a graveside service in addition to a funeral and a viewing, and rental of every limousine in the fleet. Finally, the funeral director was overcome by the idea he was taking advantage of the poor woman. He laid his hand on hers and said as gently as he could manage, "Ma'am, I know you want the best for your husband, but we would never want anyone to put themselves in a difficult financial position over a funeral."

The widow sat up straight, looked him in the eye, and said, "You just worry about what I tell you to, young man. My finances are my concern."

The day of the viewing, the funeral director confessed, the widow was dressed to the nines, her hair perfect, and her appearance transformed. The elderly couple, it turned out, was very wealthy. Having spent the last week at her husband's death bed, the widow hadn't had an opportunity to care for herself while she cared for her husband. My friend told me it was one of the most valuable lessons of his life.

Assumptions and generalizations are almost unavoidably part of life for a funeral director. In few industries are generational, socioeconomic, and racial trends so closely observed and integrated into a day's work. People outside the business are often surprised by the frankness with which mortuary owners talk about the "Black" or "Hispanic" funeral home in this or that part of the city. Perhaps it's because death so often reflects life, and a funeral director only has a few days in which to work, leaving no time for political correctness or nuance. Perhaps it's because the funeral is one of the last remaining traditions still so heavily affected by affluence, religion, and ethnicity. For a funeral director who sees how starkly a Greek Orthodox funeral differs from an African American crowning ceremony or an atheist celebration of life, it seems impossible (and in some cases counterproductive) to avoid making assumptions based on clients' backgrounds.

For all of death care's meticulous attention to its customer at the micro level, and for all its understanding of social trends and evolving demographics at the macro level, there's a detail (a weakness, in fact) about today's funeral customers that seems to have been missed—or at least misunderstood. And that vulnerability might provide a clue that will help us understand how to better serve core clients and prospects for another generation.

In Mie Prefecture, Japan, there is a shrine known as Ise Jingu. According to some, the shrine is more than 2,000 years old. It's a treasured monument for the Japanese people. So valuable, in fact, that they regularly destroy it.

Every twenty years, in a ceremony called Shinkinen Sengo, the Ise shrine is meticulously deconstructed and then rebuilt by the local community.[1] The regular rebuilding is the secret to the shrine's longevity. The Long Now Foundation writes that the shrine hasn't survived because of "heroic engineering or structural overkill, but rather cultural continuity."[2] In other words, when historic buildings are lost in the West, they're often lost forever because the knowledge of how to rebuild them disappears with the structure itself. But by rebuilding Ise Jingu every generation, the

Japanese ensure that the structure never outlives the memory of how to create it—and therefore that it can always be rebuilt.

Ise Jingu is a powerful metaphor for cultural know-how. And it's a perfect picture of the challenge presented for the contemporary mortuary in serving its target audience.

In the late 1990s, the U.S. Institute of Medicine's Committee on Care at the End of Life issued a now-widely read report on improving end-of-life care. It observed a phenomenon that funeral directors at that time already knew by experience, and that they know even better two decades later:

> For most of human history…dying—like being born—was generally a family, communal, and religious event, not a medical one. Because many deaths occurred at home, people were likely to care for dying relatives and, thus, to have a fairly personal and direct experience with dying and death. In the United States, death at home in the care of family has been widely superseded by an institutional, professional, and technological process of dying. That process—its positive aspects notwithstanding—has distanced the final stage of life from the rest of living.[3]

In other words, because of the evolution of medical care, we have crossed the threshold into new territory. The first generation of Americans is now living without any knowledge of how to "rebuild the shrine." Because of this "institutional, professional, and technological process of dying," Americans are isolated from the process of death and dying, whereas just a few generations ago, death would have been unavoidable, occurring with relative frequency in their homes and the homes of close friends and family.[4] Moreover, people are, perhaps for the first time in human history, planning funerals and navigating close personal losses later in life and without any earlier exposure to or "practice" with death. While the *Approaching Death* report highlights one particular reason for this phenomenon, it is in fact a perfect storm. A confluence of multiple factors have aligned to suddenly obliterate our cultural literacy on death.

On one level, the phenomenon is purely a mathematical one. When people only lived into their fifties or sixties, one would simply be exposed to more death more frequently.[5] If people don't live as long, it's more difficult to avoid a loss. If Grandma only lives to be sixty, then you'll have to bury her in your teens or twenties. But if she lives to be ninety-five, then you might be well into your fifties yourself before you're ever confronted with the loss of a grandparent.

In the past century, life expectancy in the United States has increased by nearly 50 percent—people live more than 24 years longer on average today than they did a century ago.[6] This trend has had an unprecedented effect on our exposure to death and dying. It is no doubt to be celebrated that we can live longer, more comfortable lives. But an unintended side effect of this longevity has been declining "death literacy." We're simply less exposed to death, and the exposure we do get is later in life, making it of diminished value in training and preparing for more immediate and painful deaths, like those of a spouse or parent.

In fact, there's arguably a kind of "negative training" taking place. Simply by virtue of spending our first decades without ever attending a funeral, we might predispose ourselves to believe that death is theoretical and avoidable. A young woman who has attended dozens of family members' funerals by the time she is in her fifties is no doubt better prepared and less shell-shocked when she must bury her parents than a woman for whom the loss of a parent is her very first experience with death.

Over the same period, as the "Approaching Death" report explains, nursing homes and "outsourced" care for the elderly have even further distanced people from the process of dying.[7] Nursing homes in their modern iteration didn't exist until the mid-twentieth century and have only become commonplace in the last few decades. The passage of Medicare and Medicaid in 1965 made contemporary nursing homes possible,[8] and the number of nursing home beds increased by more than 300 percent from 1960 to 1976 alone.[9] By 2000, nursing homes had become a hundred-billion-dollar industry.[10]

Today, half of Americans over age 95 live in some kind of skilled nursing or assisted living facility, compared to only one percent of the population aged 65-74.[11] This statistic represents two simultaneous trends: first, that nursing homes are becoming more prevalent and are housing a greater percentage of Americans than ever before; and second, that Americans are vastly more likely to live in a nursing home as they approach mortality. These two trends together reinforce what we already know to be true. Americans are simply less exposed to death than they were historically. Today, a loved one is likely to die in the presence of facility staff in a nursing home, or in a hospital setting, rather than at home in the presence of friends and family.

If the process of dying has been outsourced over the past century, so too has the process of handling the dead. Until the mid-1800s there were no funeral directors. Prior to the nineteenth century, families would care for their own dead at home, having nobody to do it for them. That's the way it was done for millennia, from the Roman Empire to Old World Europe to the American Frontier. The Civil War, and the need to transport bodies over long distances, created the demand for modern embalming practices.[12] Funeral directors wouldn't even be recognized as a real profession for another half-century.[13] After demand fell off following the Civil War, embalming wouldn't become common practice again until the turn of the century.

In other words, we've recently crossed yet another threshold. For the first time in history, people have no memories of caring for the dead themselves. An extensive write-up in *The New York Times* highlighted the growing interest in in-home care for the body, but this remains a novelty practiced only by a tiny fraction of the bereaved.[14] A local news story in 2017 covered a Kentucky family who had to dig their grandmother's grave when the cemetery neglected its duties.[15] The article captured the family's (rightful) indignation, but seemed to overlook the fact that until very recently, this difficult experience would have been commonplace.

In fact, we are only a generation or two removed—especially in more rural parts of the country—from people who would have remembered all these novelties being common practice. Grandma would have died at home, would have been prepared by her loved ones at home, would have been viewed and mourned at home, and likely would have been buried not too far from home. Today, we're accustomed to having professionals relieve us of those duties. And because we don't remember anything else, we see that service as a given—something that we can take for granted—rather than a miraculous innovation that frees us from a less-pleasant default position.

Other societal trends, too, have chipped away at our knowledge base when it comes to remembering how to "rebuild the shrine." Religion, certainly in the Western tradition, brings its own focus on mortality. Funerals often occur in churches, and church can provide a weekly reminder of human frailty that makes death a little less surprising. Pew Research has noted that more than 56 million adult Americans are now religiously unaffiliated, a figure that grew by more than a third in less than a decade and that now outnumbers both Catholics and mainline Protestants.[16] This rise of the so-called "Nones" represents an unprecedented step away from a framework and community proximate to mortality.

It's not just churches. Institutions generally have fallen out of favor over the last half-century. Boomers have a notorious predilection against institutions—so much so that it's almost a punchline. But the stereotype is rooted in reality. Marriage rates in the U.S. began to steadily decline (a trend that has yet to reverse) in 1980, when Boomers would have been expected to be at peak marrying age.[17] No-fault divorce, too, came with the Boomer generation, the first such law redefining the weight of marriage having being passed in California in 1970.[18] The Boomers are notorious for record divorce rates over the same period.[19] Declines in organizational membership have closely followed the era in which Boomers were reaching adulthood. Even community and civic organizations like Rotary International have famously suffered dwindling membership as the Boomers have succeeded their parents.[20] Each of these trends has cemented the troubling notion that the community, formality, and tradition of a funeral are downright archaic.

Researcher Lyman Stone notes an interesting phenomenon over the same period. While Boomers are notoriously anti-institution, they spent their heyday "locking down" institutions for their benefit.[21] Describing what he calls "institutional aging," Stone notes that "the political ascendency of the Boomers brought with it tightening control and strict regulation."[22] From land-use and zoning laws to licensing and regulatory requirements for businesses (the percentage of American workers who must hold a license to do their jobs has risen from less than 5 to more than 25 percent since 1950[23]), Boomers have presided over a period of intense restriction and codification. In other words, the Boomers didn't only abandon or resist institutions, they hard-wired them to their own tastes and preferences, making laws stricter and jobs harder for future generations to adapt or rewire for their own purposes. The generation under which America became more anti-institution also made those same institutions less flexible and adaptable.

These paradoxical trends—declining trust in institutions alongside slowing evolution of those institutions—capture the funeral home's dilemma: fewer Americans want a traditional funeral, but thanks to the Funeral Rule, state regulations, and the massive overhead burden of traditional mortuaries, funeral homes find themselves disincentivized (or outright restricted) from evolving. Therefore, subsequent generations increasingly perceive funeral homes as outdated, stale, and irrelevant.

It doesn't add up to a pretty picture. Americans today are less exposed to death at earlier ages, robbing them of valuable opportunities to "learn death" from prior generations. When deaths do occur, they're often in clinical rather than familial settings, further distancing and alienating survivors from the experience. Modern Americans have never had to handle a body themselves, meaning they're less appreciative of those who do it for them. And even apart from death, people are trending against institutions like religion, which might remind them of and prepare them for their own mortality. They've also been prone to reject formal community structures, from marriage to Rotary, which lend some context and preparation for community grief in the shape of a funeral. And if that wasn't enough, the regulatory environment is stacked in such a way that the very institutions they so distrust are straightjacketed against change.

No wonder you're tired.

On one level, all this should be terrifying. Death care professionals have historically succeeded when people understood them, knew their role, and were comfortable (even predisposed) to purchase the goods and services they provided. Today they find themselves picking up after a perfect storm that has demolished all these advantages. If there were a little shop in Japan that perennially sold the supplies needed to rebuild the shrine every twenty years, it would do a reliable (though intermittent) business. But if everybody suddenly gave up on the tradition and quit rebuilding the shrine, you would expect that shop to go out of business overnight. It's easy to look at the more sobering indicators around funeral service—skyrocketing cremation rates, plummeting chapel usage, declining averages—and conclude that this is the very thing that is happening today. People have forgotten how to rebuild the shrine, and our little shop that was once a sure thing is now suffering mightily as a result.

But there's another way to look at it. If our hypothetical Japanese hardware store was a family business, we might expect the family members, over the years, to have learned how to build the shrine themselves. After all, knowing how many of a particular part to order every twenty years might go hand-in-hand with knowing that part's actual function. At the very least, that knowledge would provide some clues as to what inputs and resources are required for successful shrine-building. In fact, outside of the villagers doing the work themselves, you would expect the shopkeepers to be the world's foremost experts on shrine-building. And if some tragedy befell the local town such that nobody remembered how to do the necessary rebuilding, you would instinctively look to the shopkeepers to help you figure out what to do next. In that scenario, the shopkeepers don't go out of business; instead, they become exponentially *more* valuable, selling their consultative services and expertise for the community's collective good, rather than simply selling products the current generation has forgotten how to use.

The modern funeral home, therefore, has a unique opportunity before it. Your target audience has forgotten how to "do" death. On the one hand, that means they do not even know when to call you or what to ask for. But this is a minor concern compared to the massive opportunity in front of you. Never in human history has there been a generation so desperately in need of a death expert.

This is why I cringe any time I hear well-meaning funeral directors talk about "educating" families. If people are already unwilling to spend the time, money, and energy required for a healthy funeral, asking them to allow you to educate them only adds to a burden they've already decided not to bear.

Customers are woefully uneducated about death, to be sure, but no business model has succeeded by educating its target. Businesses succeed when they meet a demand. The demand may be spoken loudly or may be barely perceptible, but finding a product a customer will reliably pay for is hard enough—a business sets itself a mile back if it insists on selling a product that customers must be educated into buying. Nobody had a notion of what a smartphone could do until Steve Jobs handed them one.

But he didn't "educate the public" about his product's many uses; he built a product that met needs the public had been unable to articulate. For funeral service to succeed, it must do the same.

All of the social forces that have led families to resist mortuaries make them just as resistant to education about mortuaries. If I don't want to think about death, if I don't value the work of the funeral business, and if I think I can avoid death, then I don't have any interest whatsoever in being educated about death. It's like a pastor thinking that more people would come to his church if he could just educate them about theology. That may be true, but their lack of interest in theology is what keeps them out of church in the first place. If education could solve the industry's crisis, there wouldn't be a crisis.

But even more importantly, the "we just need to educate them" mentality is wrong because it squanders an opportunity. Your education— what you know about death that they do not—should be your *product*, not an ad for it. A half-century ago, funeral directors sold products because the community already understood what to do with them, much like auto parts stores sold equipment to people more or less skilled to conduct their own auto maintenance. As we have seen, our culture and economy have shifted tremendously since that time. Yet funeral directors continue to try to sell products that nobody knows what to do with anymore.

So, if you have cases of 5W-30 to sell, you can try desperately to explain to people how to change their own oil. Or you can open an oil change service business and do it for them (and sell lots of oil in the process).

Given the option between learning a new skill and letting an expert do it for them, the vast majority of people will choose the simpler option; that's how accountants, lawyers, and plumbers make a living. Today, you don't spend money at the mechanic merely for the mechanic's time or strength—you spend it for his expertise. Really, you're spending it so that you don't have to learn as much about your car as he already knows.

Economist Peter Drucker coined the term "knowledge economy"[24] to refer to a broader societal pattern (which has coincided with the Information Age) through which work has become less about the traffic of tangible goods and more about intangible knowledge and expertise. That doesn't mean products go away, which is important for mortuaries. Just as the Industrial Revolution didn't end farming (because people still need to eat), the Information Age won't end products (because people still need to buy things). The idea of a knowledge economy for death care is less about getting rid of products (though we will talk about that in Chapters 7 and 10) and more about focusing on what you know. This requires a shift: thinking of your knowledge as *intrinsically* valuable, rather than as simply a means by which to sell a product.

The families you serve are primed for this, which presents an opportunity. They're used to subscribing to all kinds of apps and services where they're essentially paying for knowledge—the knowledge of a coder here, or a fitness expert there—to help them think through a process they don't want to spend time on, or to help them understand dynamics they don't want to study. The idea of paying for knowledge and expertise would have been unusual to your companies' first families a century ago. But fortunately for you, it is a familiar, common concept for Boomers—and even more so for their children, who are just starting to make their parents' funeral arrangements.

As Boomers and their children die, American funeral homes have a tough case to make. Nobody cares about the brass tacks of funeral service anymore. Once, lifting the burden of burial and coordination off of a grieving family was a novelty. They expected to have to do it themselves, and they'd pay a premium for somebody to come in and save the day. Those days are over. Your core offerings are commoditized expectations, rather than groundbreaking innovations. But you're providing expertise within the knowledge economy, whether you know it or not.

Consider the "first call." Fifty years ago, when a family called a funeral home, it was to begin to make arrangements, or maybe to do a little price-shopping. Today it's something different altogether. Families might wrap it in the guise of those things, but in reality what they're doing is getting their bearings. Remember, you're talking to people with little or no exposure to death, who are utterly uneducated regarding what to do, what steps to take, or even what's appropriate. They call you because you're the expert. For a few minutes, and for free, they can glean some valuable information.

It actually starts sooner than that. In preparing a research project for a client, my firm discovered that Google searches abound for terms like "what to do when someone dies,"[25] "how much does cremation cost,"[26] planning a "celebration of life,"[27] and even "grief resources."[28] The families you serve don't have anyone to ask about these things. So they're asking their phones.

Or, look at aftercare. The traditional grief process happens in a week—viewing, funeral, graveside, opening, closing, done. Every touchpoint after that is often considered a marketing investment to "retain" a lead. But here, too, you're providing valuable expertise; those families desperately need guidance and support through the entire process. And here, again, you're the seasoned expert, having met with thousands of families over the course of your career.

Challenged to increase cemetery revenue by our client Sunset Memorial Park, my firm invented "Scatter Day," a concept that has since taken root across the country. We discovered through our research that a significant percentage of American households have unwanted cremated remains at home. We set up and heavily advertised a local holiday when families could bring their loved ones' remains "out of the shadows" and receive both a cenotaph and a scattering, free of charge. For those families looking for other options (we surmised, again correctly, that the real barrier was taboo and guilt, not price) we would have team members on hand to make arrangements.

The outpouring of appreciation was overwhelming. One couple sobbed with relief, finally laying their son to rest fully two decades after his passing. The cemetery received calls and letters of gratitude for months after the fact. And the revenue was just as noteworthy. The advertising budget for the event had been substantial, yet we were revenue-positive even before the big day because there was so much pent-up demand. The lesson is clear: If you are assuming that your opportunity to guide families in grief ends the day after they make arrangements, you're leaving money (and opportunities to serve) on the table.

Here, cemeterians are the experts. It's rare for a funeral director to engage with a family after the service, though there are those sweet moments when a family will return and ask for a specific funeral director because she cared for them so well years or even decades prior. But a cemeterian sees families return to a grave day after day, year after year, providing a valuable insight into the longevity of grief. Mortuaries and cemeteries alike would do well not to negate the efforts of grief counselors, and even funeral directors, who seek opportunities to serve families long after a loss has occurred. By doing so you will provide a valuable service, and likely even a profitable one.

Clearly, the world has changed. Your prospect finds herself in a position quite different indeed from those of the families your grandparents served. Yet this does not make the situation hopeless—it simply means new models must be considered and new value points must be offered. Funeral homes must be willing to leave old assumptions behind and continually look to reinvent the business model around the evolving needs of the family. That might mean simple changes, and it might mean some that are quite drastic—not merely adding new products to the lineup but rethinking the product altogether. But if these changes to models are grounded in mission and moral imperative, they will not be haphazard shots in the dark. Instead, they will be calculated moves to realign your business around grieving families who have forgotten you—and who need you more than ever.

Chapter 3
Nonreligious Green Burials on Mars

Winston Churchill once quipped that "nothing in life is so exhilarating as to be shot at without result."[1] If that's true in battle, it's equally true in business. To be attacked for years, or decades, by an onslaught of new criticisms and new competitors, and to emerge successful (and profitable) year after year, is exhilarating. And it's difficult to conceive of an industry that has been shot at so much as funeral service.

To be sure, the business isn't what it used to be. Trends from the spread of Mitfordism to the ascendency of cremation to the rise of the Nones have all taken their toll. Funeral care is no longer the hyper-profitable investment that it was in the '80s. But many of the professionals I talk with today are feeling pretty good. They're still doing a reliable business. Many are optimistic about the future. Overwhelmingly, as measured by both anecdotal and quantitative data, funeral directors express confidence in their current model.

In fact, as my firm has studied the death care business through the context of what we call the Disruption Cycle, practitioners overwhelmingly classify themselves far more optimistically than the outside evidence would suggest. All businesses, and all industries, can be mapped to one of five phases: Acceleration, Maturation, Saturation, Commoditization, and Disruption. It's a self-evident lifecycle: you start, grow rapidly, find your footing, and then new entrants come in and bring new challenges and pressures until what was once a new invention becomes a commodity, competing at the margins until the category is disrupted again. Fast food was in the acceleration phase when McDonalds pioneered the concept. Today it's a commodity. Travel agents once commanded solid prices when they were a mature business. Today, they're a commodity, effortlessly replaced by smartphones and travel apps.

Funeral service faces declining demand, mounting margin pressures, the proliferation of price shopping and cost-driven options, and a generally low public perception of the industry. All evidence indicates that the modern mortuary is a commoditized business ripe for disruption—near the end of the lifecycle. But on average, funeral directors and mortuary owners routinely classify themselves as barely into the Saturation phase—only about halfway through the cycle. In other words, the bullets are flying, but those on the inside are confident that it will be without result—and they are feeling like exhilarated survivors.

What's going on?

FIGURE 3.1: SELF-IDENTIFICATION OF
FUNERAL PROFESSIONALS ON THE DISRUPTION CYCLE

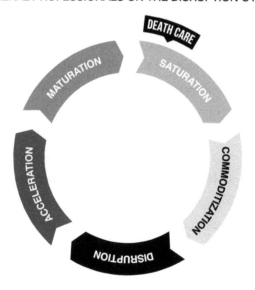

When I first heard of Solace Cremation, I thought it was a death knell for traditional funeral homes. Research conducted by my firm had indicated that the real itch scratched by direct cremation is simplicity, not savings. In other words, consumers want direct cremation not just to save money, but to streamline the experience and sidestep traditional mortuaries. Direct cremation outlets have largely missed this and are generally focused on offering a cheap option rather than the simple one customers are after. So Solace, with its sleek user experience, a 100 percent online offering, and an injection of high-end creative leadership (the firm was founded by two former Nike creative directors[2]), seemed to offer just what the doctor ordered.

The very next week, I learned about Tulip, another company—this one heralded as "Silicon Valley's no-frills journey to cremation"[3]—with the same concept. It seemed the challengers were gaining traction.

But as I discussed the concepts with funeral directors in the know, they were less than impressed. One owner of a very widely known (and very innovative) funeral home reminded me that these companies have come and gone for decades. They always promise transformation, and so far, none of them have delivered.

He had a point.

Costco sells caskets, but it has done so since 2004.[4] Your casket sales might not be what they used to be, but that's hardly due to Costco entering the market—which is why when Amazon and Walmart hopped on the same bandwagon, it was perceived more as a hassle for funeral homes than a credible threat.

LifeGems, the now-ubiquitous company offering to turn cremated remains into diamonds, was launched in 2002. It was heralded at the time (and has been since) as a transformative new way to handle death, but it has hardly delivered on that promise.[5] Instead, it simply provides one more merchandise offering for mortuaries to display alongside racks of other jewelry options like Legacy Touch—one more opportunity to provide revenue as interest in other offerings starts to wane.

The sheer volume of supposed "disruptions" to the death business is overwhelming. It seems that every year brings more entrants to the industry, from every direction imaginable.

Death doulas and midwives represent a cottage industry comprised of numerous local companies (mostly sole proprietorships) with no less than two international trade associations.[6] Funeral consultants represent a similar, but distinct, approach. Some, like Empowered Widow, are companies driven largely by a single individual, while others, like Going in Style, use a franchise model, allowing others to set themselves up as funeral consultants with low barriers to entry and minimal startup costs.[7]

Funeral concierge companies like Everest, which grew in partnership with a life insurance firm, offer to simplify and streamline the process of selecting end-of-life companies—the "Travelocity" of death.[8] Funeralocity sprung up quickly, even its name alluding to convenience-oriented tech companies in parallel verticals.[9] FuneralDecisions.com ("Helping thousands of families compare since 2008"), Final Moments Concierge Services, and Funerals360 all represent concierge models.[10]

Online-only models, like Solace and Tulip, have proliferated around the country. These often seek to eliminate overhead by partnering with an existing funeral home and operating on the back-end as a lead generation service. This offers an appealing-yet-risky revenue source for local mortuaries eager to offset high overhead investments. SimpleCremationOnline, Basic Funerals and Cremation Choices, and others in their vein are the digital generation of the funeral alternative and "cremation society" pop-ups of earlier decades.[11]

Preplanning, too, is facing new digital entrants. Moving beyond the specifics of funeral planning, new firms are offering to organize, catalog, and manage all sorts of end-of-life details, from funeral planning to wills to passwords for banking and online accounts. Cake, Gyst, Everplans,

AfterNote, FuneralWise, Beyond, DyingMatters.org, the Digital Legacy Association, the Digital Beyond, Postumo, Ghost Memo, and LifeNaut all offer various forms and degrees of postmortem documentation[12]— some even going so far as to promise "to explore the transfer of human consciousness to computers/robots and beyond."[13]

A global trend toward sustainability has generated its share of products and business concepts in the death care space. The Natural Death Centre and the Green Burial Council bemoan the volumes of wood, steel, concrete, and chemicals buried each year as part of the interment process.[14] Green casket companies like the Natural Burial Company, Passages International, and ARKA offer everything from wicker to corrugated cardboard to "Ecopods" made of recycled paper as alternatives to traditional caskets.[15] Coeio sells an "Infinity burial suit" with integrated fungal spores at $1,500, designed to "return bodies to the earth respectfully, affordably, and without damaging the environment."[16] Capsula Mundi lets you inter your loved one within the roots of a sapling tree—a similar concept to that offered by The Living Urn company.[17, 18] Biodegradable urns are available from a wide variety of sources. Eternal Reefs, structured as a charitable organization, will help you bury your loved one at sea. It offers "permanent living legacies that memorialize the passing of a loved one by helping to preserve and protect the marine environment for the benefit of future generations."[19]

Even cremation now has alternatives. Recompose is a company focused on "natural organic reduction,"[20] a process that is now legal in Washington State. Alkaline hydrolysis, also known as aquamation, water cremation, or resomation, is now available and legal in many states.[21]

Ash scattering services are an industry unto themselves, with companies offering to scatter ashes for you at precise GPS coordinates (with a certificate to boot).[22] The Eternal Ascent Society and A Journey With Wings offer aerial scatterings.[23] Elysium Space and Celestis will go even farther and launch your loved one into space.[24] Heavens Above Fireworks offers pyrotechnics services that include cremated remains within a fire-works display.[25] My Holy Smoke will pack your cremated remains into shotgun shells for a final salute.[26] And CremationSolutions.com features "The Loved One Launcher," which "will shoot earthly remains over seventy feet into the air!"[27]

These new models and companies have their fans. In fact, the PR around disruption of funeral care has become a genre all its own. *Forbes* wrote in 2019 that the "Death Concierge" was going to "elevate the nature of dying from 'death' to 'celebration.'"[28] *Vox* announced the same year that "Disruption comes for death,"[29] and recited a catalog of eco-friendly offerings as evidence that traditional burials would be replaced by innovative new concepts. *The New York Times* published a 9,000-word article in 2019 heralding in great and emotional detail the rise of DIY death care, positioning in-home alternatives to mortuaries as the new wave of the future.[30]

But in practice, funeral homes are not yet losing significant chunks of revenue to all these "disruptions." Relatively few families express interest in them at all. Why? How can so many bullets have been fired at the heart of this industry while "the way we've always done it" remains a reliable and even successful approach?

It might not be as remarkable—nor as reassuring—as it seems.

For one, disruption is not a catch-all for innovation. Disruption can be defined as "a disturbance or problem which interrupts an event, activity, or process."[31] For the most part, new startups in the funeral space have not presented "problems" that "interrupt" contemporary funeral homes. On the contrary, they are simply new revenue streams intended to fit neatly within the status quo.

Calling new green burial options "disruptive" is like calling a local fleet operator a disruptor because it bought new vehicles with better gas mileage. Disruption tends to upend the current situation entirely, not staple onto it. Amazon is an outright alternative to Sears—and one that pushed its competitor over the edge into bankruptcy. You don't ask your travel agent to use Travelocity for you; you use it to bypass him. The automobile didn't make horses faster, cleaner, and more efficient; it replaced them entirely. Unless a new offering or business model threatens the core of your business, it's not disruptive.

So, when *Vox*, *The New York Times*, and *Forbes* are quick to announce the arrival of death care disruptors, they are playing fast and loose with the definition of disruption. New product lines sold via mortuaries fail the disruption litmus test. They are reliant on the status quo, so they're certainly not going to buck it. Even alternatives like Tulip are not as disruptive as they seem on the surface. Tulip operated at its inception by letting local mortuaries carry its overhead costs, so mortuary owners (at least in the short term) were able to treat it as a new revenue stream rather than as a competitor.

In fact, many of these so-called disruptors are not only not disrupting, they may actually be calcifying existing habits. With cremation rates on the rise and funeral homes generally (though often not specifically) facing turbulence, I frequently ask funeral home owners how they're doing with innovation. Often their answers betray a sense of false security. I have yet to speak with a funeral home owner (usually while we're standing in a lobby that could be a set for a 1930s period film) who doesn't think of himself as an innovator. Again, the industry has been shot at but hasn't taken a bullet yet. This is not only exhilarating; it can lead to the delusion that you're bulletproof.

My firm's national research further confirms this unsettling misplaced confidence. In a nationwide study of hundreds of mortuaries conducted in partnership with Selected Independent Funeral Homes, 66 percent of funeral home professionals claimed that their competitive differentiation is growing.[32] Only 21 percent agree that they don't know their place in a changing marketplace.[33] Four out of five say they take creative risks.[34] Funeral home owners nationally are feeling confident, and they're congratulating themselves on their achievements.

What's concerning here is that the picture painted by the industry is so sharply at odds with the portrait its customers are seeing.[35] For more than a decade, my firm has also been conducting market research among mortuary consumers, starting with the funeral industry's first national segmentation study. Our research has consistently indicated that the vast majority of funeral home consumers are not the conventional, religious psychographic for whom the business model is built.[36] These traditional groups actually represent a minority nationally—only 33 percent.[37] The rest are not fans of funeral homes. Some wish they could plan a funeral without having to come into a space they see as dated and anachronistic. Most think funeral care is overpriced. Many are suspicious of funeral directors. But 67 percent of your customers are at some point or another on Mitford's spectrum of trying to avoid your offerings, whether by acting defensively when they come in to make arrangements or by actively seeking out direct cremation alternatives.

What that means is that two thirds of the population effectively lies outside the spectrum of a traditional funeral home's prospective customer base.[38] Of course, the specifics of this reality vary greatly by geography and by definition, but the idea is straightforward: most people are dissatisfied with what is being sold. Focus groups have revealed even more poignant insight: those who tend not to place value on traditional funerals and funeral home offerings are often outright hostile, associating funerals and funeral directors with their worst experiences, with incidents of bigotry or exclusion, and with their bitterest memories of family and organized religion. It's no surprise that the people with negative feelings toward traditional institutions are not the biggest fans of their local funeral home, but what's striking is how closely they link you to their other negative experiences.

Moreover, when polled or studied in focus groups, even the tried-and-true customer base tends toward less than favorable views of mortuaries. Even in population segments that believe (for instance) that funerals are necessary for the grieving process, there is a general distrust and discomfort toward funeral homes. My firm has (very successfully) used statistical algorithms to segment the population according to their perceptions and attitudes toward funerals and traditional funeral care services.[39] But when we interviewed even the most *favorable* segment in a focus group and asked them to name the first word that came to mind when they thought of funeral homes, "cost," "pressure," and "thieves" were among the terms thrown around. Again, these are not fringe, antiestablishment folks. These are religious, older, traditional, conservative people who attend funerals frequently and agree that funerals are important.

If customer perception matched industry perception, then direct cremation wouldn't be on the rise. After all, direct cremation is widely understood by funeral homes and the public alike as an alternative to the services of a mortuary. So if the future is sunny and customer relationships are solid, you would expect to see cremation rates dropping as people line up to pay more for traditional funerals.

But if those aren't the trends your business is seeing, it's possible that the picture isn't quite as rosy as you might like to believe. And even though *Forbes*, *Vox*, and others have created a narrative that funeral homes have survived an onslaught of fierce attackers, the reality is that the real threats have yet to materialize. Either way, it should be concerning that so many enemies are gathering at your gates.

Think about the last time you expressed frustration over a particular company, or thought to yourself, "There has to be a better way." Chances are it was a situation where you felt cornered, where there was no viable alternative, but you had to bite the bullet anyway—perhaps working with an attorney (and receiving an exorbitant hourly bill) or going to a doctor and waiting hours for a five-minute examination. We all fantasize about finding an alternative. And when one makes it to the market, people often abandon the status quo in droves. TurboTax saved millions of Americans from the confusion, fear, and expense of the traditional filing process—and few have looked back.

Why, then, if customers are distrustful and new challengers are plentiful, has funeral service remained relatively unscathed? There are several reasons.

The simplest and most obvious is that demand for disruption hasn't yet climaxed. Boomers—that monolithic, anti-institutional generation—were born between 1946 and 1964. The youngest of them won't reach the age of average life expectancy until 2042. Even the oldest have only recently begun to reach that mark. So far, we have only buried (or more likely, cremated) the first of the Boomers. To be sure, Boomers have already made some mark planning funerals for their parents, but "what Dad would have wanted" still holds sway. The more traditional, institutional Greatest Generation is still making its mark in the products and services that funeral homes offer. That will be a very different story in another decade.

Death is the last thing you do in life, and death is the last institution that will be reshaped by Baby Boomers. While we've begun to see those impacts, the wave has yet to come ashore. So if you're continuing to do well with traditional offerings today, you might hold off a few more years before congratulating yourself on having weathered the storm.

But this might not be the most important reason that none of the bullets fired at funeral service have found their mark. It's not because funeral homes are bulletproof or have a bulletproof business model (far from it). Rather, it is because, so far, you've only been shot at by poor marksmen.

Without exception, the successful and disruptive entrants to any industry—the ones that topple the reigning champions—are those that empathize best with the customer. Music streaming services like Spotify have eliminated the time, cost, and difficulty of acquiring a music library or exploring new artists. Starbucks recognized the consistency and comfort of your local coffee shop and took it international: no more guessing or relearning a menu. Google boiled the complexity of the entire internet down to a single keyword box. Businesses win when they empathize with their customers.

Uber intentionally developed a product in response to the shortcomings of San Francisco's taxi business. Every attribute of the business was engineered around "getting in the back of the cab" with a perspective of empathy toward the customer. Cab companies have a million excuses why everything in a taxi is the way it is: it's a tough business with high overhead, complicated regulations, and serious demands on labor and capital. That's why nothing ever changed; the business model was built around the business' challenges, not the customer's needs.

But when Travis Kalanick and Garrett Camp sat in the back of a taxi in 2009 and viewed the experience through customers' eyes, all they saw were opportunities.[40] How do we make finding a ride more convenient? How do we incentivize good customer service? How do we hold drivers accountable and improve quality of experience? How can we make it easier to pay? By building their model around what the customer needed, they were able to blow the doors off of the existing business model.

Truly disruptive businesses have two superpowers: the empathy to understand the customer's needs and the expertise to meet those needs. Uber succeeded by having both—plenty of frustrated travelers surely sat in the back of a cab and thought, "There ought to be a better way," but lacked the vision, capital, interest, knowledge of startups, or software expertise to make the idea a reality.

The reason the status quo has lasted so long in death care is not because funeral homes and cemeteries are invincibly outstanding at doing what they do. It's simply because no challenger has yet brought both criteria to the table.

The majority of new competitors, in fact, offer neither. Cannons for shooting cremains into the air aren't built out of empathy for the customer nor out of an expertise on serving families; they're just gimmicks offered by those looking to capitalize on the existing infrastructure. Most death care "disruptions" fall into this category. Dinner plates made out of cremated remains, biodegradable urns, and fireless cremation are all solutions in search of a problem. A family here or there might have particular concerns about the environmental impacts of a burial, or a particularly creative memorial product might scratch the itch for an especially artistic family, but, by and large, the new entrants to the death care space are addressing ancillary challenges. None of these products get to the heart of the disconnects and frustrations that are driving a wedge between funeral homes and families.

A helpful exercise here might be to leaf through *The American Way of Death* or to write down a list of the most common complaints heard about funeral homes. Any funeral director could do this almost from memory. Then ask yourself to name a product or competitor that genuinely addresses or solves any of these problems. Normally, in the case of disruptive businesses, the overlap between the list of grievances and the solutions offered by the product is uncanny. But funeral service, to date, has no such overlap. The common complaints remain unaddressed by newcomers and old-timers alike, as they have for nearly six decades.

There are a few innovations which pass the first criterion. To be sure, both Jessica Mitford and countless families since have complained about the expense of a funeral, and especially about not wanting to pay for all the extras. Low-cost funeral homes and direct cremation societies arose in direct response to this need. In that regard, they are empathetic business models.

Similarly, Tulip and Solace demonstrate empathy as they respond directly and clearly to those frustrated with the outdated clumsiness of the funeral planning process. Today, I can do almost anything online. If all I want is a direct cremation, why should I have to drive in, make arrangements, sit in an inherently uncomfortable place for two hours to hear a sales pitch and answer questions that could have been addressed online, only to have to make another trip in to pick up death certificates and cremated remains once they're ready? The offer to simplify, stream-line, and automate the experience is an excellent and direct response to customer demand.

The problem is that neither of these innovations go far enough. Amazon didn't just make retail cheaper; it made it cheaper *and* more convenient *and* faster *and* more accountable *and* more customizable. Chipotle didn't just offer a better-tasting option for fast food; it improved taste, addressed health concerns, eliminated complexity, reinvented ex-perience, tapped into the environmentalist zeitgeist, and reshaped res-taurant staffing norms. Word processing software made typing easier, re-defined the editing process, improved accessibility and convenience, and cut paper and ink costs.

Disruption is impressive. But part of what's so alluring about it is that it's really difficult to achieve. To take a litany of customer complaints and have the creativity, objectivity, and tenacity to address them with a new model outside the traditional way is not something that happens every day. In death care, it's something that has yet to happen at all.

Usually, addressing so many challenges simultaneously requires some specialized expertise, which is why the second superpower (the abil-ity to really meet customer needs) is important. Funeral customers don't *just* want cheap cremation; they want to be free of all of the upselling and productization that makes funeral planning uncomfortable. They want guidance through an experience for which they're unprepared and which is intrinsically disorienting. They want to know they've honored their loved one. And they want all that without having to visit a dated building they associate with pain.

Most "disruptors" in death care fail to deliver even one or two of these needs. Many funeral homes have found that low-cost cremation alone isn't financially viable, so they fall back to propping up the business with exactly the type of product sales their customers hoped to avoid. Similarly, the outsider perspective that allowed former Nike executives

Keith Crawford and David Odusanya to create a gorgeous user experience online also left them oblivious to the other needs of their target (such as a gentle guiding hand through the confusion of end-of-life planning). These "disruptions" have been more akin to an entrepreneur who heard somebody tell him about a bad cab ride than to one who has sat in the back of a hundred taxis himself.

And that's exactly why none of them have taken root. Yet. Funeral homes across America should be thankful, but not cocky, that so far they have survived an onslaught of products and services aimed at their customers. Like armies of impotent gunmen in a low-budget action film, the enemies are numerous but not remarkably effective. But that fact is distinct from the prevailing problem that the customer is tired of the usual approach, suspicious of the innumerable products, and frustrated by an out-of-date business model.

Miraculously, nobody in six decades has created a solution with the capability to address Mitford's concerns and effectively compete with traditional funeral businesses. Or maybe it's not such a miracle. If it's true that disruption requires both empathy and expertise, today's funeral professionals might be the only people with the know-how to build the model that's needed. And so far, they've lacked the imminent threat that would incentivize them to tear down their existing house and build a better one. As the Boomers age and as disturbing trends solidify into norms, that incentive might be coming.

Whether it comes from within or without, funeral care will be disrupted. No business model lasts forever. It's difficult to predict when the disruption will happen, or how many fads will come and go before real disruption occurs. Something about the macabre nature of death care seems to lay down a gauntlet for new entrants to conceive of the most bizarre offerings possible, as if the only problem to solve in death is mundanity. But it's not going to be the wacky that turns the business on its head; nonreligious green burials on Mars, when somebody offers them, will get headlines, but they won't be transformative. Transformation is going to happen the moment someone with the know-how and resources to serve the public turns to frustrated, grieving families and says,

"I hear you. I understand what you're asking for. And I'm going to give it to you."

Chapter 4
The Right Way

"If embalming is taken out of the funeral, then viewing the body will also be lost. If viewing is lost, then the body itself will not be central to the funeral. If the body is taken out of the funeral, then what does the funeral director have to sell?"[1]

This quotation, from a letter by John Kroshus, onetime director of the University of Minnesota Mortuary Science Program, was gleefully cited by Jessica Mitford as evidence of the self-centeredness of the funeral industry. "I could not have put it better," she jeered.[2] Mitford saw embalming as the most egregious example of the industry's excess, and as the lynchpin of its existence, because of what it represented in her mind: an unnecessary aspect of the American tradition of death foisted upon families—not for the families' benefit, but for the benefit of "the funeral men."

Mitford argued fervently against the "demonstrably flimsy," "absurd," and "patently fraudulent" claims by "the funeral men" that funerals, and especially viewing of the deceased, are beneficial to the grief process.[3] She further claimed that terms like "grief therapy" were invented out of whole cloth, simply to prop up the associated revenue from embalming.[4] After all, if a viewing isn't necessary, then neither is embalming, and by Kroshus' rather ineloquent summation, that's a serious blow to the funeral director's bottom line.

It's an argument the public seems to have found compelling. The rise of direct cremation, the decreasing prevalence of funerals, gravesides, and viewings, and the popularity of "celebrations of life" all point to a paradigm shift. People are looking for alternatives to the traditional trappings of death. Historically, one's local culture or religion would dictate the process of grief. If your Catholic cousin passed away, you would expect to attend a rosary, a Catholic funeral, and a graveside at a Catholic cemetery. It wasn't a question of if, only of when. Today, one can make no such assumptions whatsoever. You wait to hear what the family decides. A traditional funeral and visitation or a ceremoniless disposition of the body are equally up for grabs. Families choose for themselves how to proceed, feeling and inventing their way along.

There's nothing inherently wrong with this individualized approach. In fact, it might be odd to expect anything else in our culture of endless customization. But it does require liberation from any objectively correct way of processing a death—something conveniently delivered by the notion that funeral directors counsel only in their own self-interest. If I desperately want to avoid exercising, then I must convince myself that doing so isn't that important to my health—something we've all done once or twice when we hit the snooze button in the morning. If I wish to avoid the painful medicine recommended by tradition via my local funeral director, I must first conclude that the best path for grieving is completely up to me—and therefore that no objectively best path exists.

I'm even further disposed to skip a workout if I'm convinced that my trainer is lying to me, and that he recommends what he does only so I keep paying him. If funeral homes push viewings only so that they can sell more embalmings and embalming fluid, or if they fabricate myths about the processes of grief and saying goodbye in order to sell more funerals, then an alternative should be desired because, after all, the guardians of the right way cannot be trusted.

In other words, if skipping all that traditional stuff is every bit as valid as participating in it, then funeral homes are optional at best, charlatans at worst, and a calling not at all.

On the other hand, if there are objectively useful activities that are of value to the bereaved, then something is lost (and indeed, families are harmed) when these important steps are skipped. To extend the metaphor, if the personal trainer really does know what he's talking about, then it might be up to me whether to skip the workout, but there will be consequences of doing so.

Therefore, the past, present, and future of death care all hinge upon the concept of a right way of approaching death. Either there is one or there is not. If there is, then funerals and viewings and burials might be important means to an important end. If there is not, then direct "no-frills" cremation, sans funeral, is just as valid, and there's little reason to spend all the extra money and hassle on the more expensive and often burdensome traditional options. I might choose the latter, but the burden of proof for *preferences* is very different than that for *needs*.

It's important to be clear on what we're talking about. To describe a "right way to grieve" is absolutely, unequivocally *not* to say that the traditional funerals of the North are superior to those of the South, or that a Christian burial is right but a Jewish one is wrong, or that an African American crowning ceremony is any less right than a Catholic burial mass. It's not even to say (and this is important) that cremation is wrong. It's not to say that burial is inherently superior to entombment, or that sitting *shiva* is "righter" than praying the rosary. In fact, the overwhelming diversity and breadth of available cultural and customary approaches to death care betray the lie that there is no right way to grieve.

Because there are as many different ways to approach grieving as there are cultures in the world, it's tempting to look at different traditions and conclude that there is no one way that is best. "Look, that Greek Orthodox funeral looks so different from that Irish Catholic wake. We can't choose between them, so there's no right way." But in reality, the opposite is true. It's not the differences amongst various traditions and approaches to death that are important, but their similarities. It's true that everybody does it differently, but *everybody does it.* Humans have almost universally agreed throughout history and across cultures that grieving requires action, community, and ritual.

In fact, it probably requires even more. Action, community, and ritual make for a good start, but you likely have your own list of ingredients for a healthy grief process that reflect your own experience and the makeup of your own community. That's a good thing, and you should embrace it. Doing grief right, like doing anything right, requires the leadership of expertise. Historically, a broad spectrum of community, cultural, and religious leaders have provided specific direction in defining the right way to say goodbye, but today's culture is trying to mourn without any such clarity. A right way exists. If you believe that, you can accept your role as an expert and again lead families, staff, and communities in defining and applying it.

This is an uphill battle, but it's one well worth fighting. Intentional, communal grief, and the overwhelming historical and anthropological evidence supporting it, contrast sharply against contemporary popular opinion. We're being told that to take a passive, disengaged or isolated approach to death (like Mitford's own direct cremation) is just as valid as the active, dynamic, and community-centric approaches to death that have dominated the human experience and which the death care profession helps to facilitate. There's no way to reach that conclusion without saying there is no right way to grieve. If this generation wants to be the first one in history to sidestep its duty of intentionally and communally mourning its dead, it must first invalidate the history, tradition and wisdom demanding that it do so.

This is why your opponents hold up examples like Kroshus' letter as damning to the industry. The promise of the calling was that funeral homes will help people do something they *have to do*. If it turns out that it's only something that funeral directors *want them to do*, then the entire transaction is reframed.

Though funeral directors and mortuary owners are hesitant to admit it, there's really no reason to have a funeral, or to trouble with end of life rituals and preparations and ceremonies and gatherings at all, if doing so is not in some respect superior to not doing so. The cost of an average funeral is a lot of money to spend purely out of respect for tradition, to say nothing of the stress and pain involved in planning and preparing for all the traditional end-of-life rituals. In fact, it's no coincidence that the period in which direct cremation has become more prevalent has been the same period in which expectations and norms around death care have loosened, becoming more relativistic and reluctant to impose any right way of doing things.

If there is no right way, and if it's every bit as fulfilling, healthy, valid, and helpful to cremate Mom and toss her in a shoebox in the garage as it is to celebrate her and lay her ceremoniously to rest, then mortuaries are certainly wasting their time. If both paths are equally valid, then there really is no justification for the entire business other than, as Kroshus admits, the self-interest of funeral directors.

Which is true? Are there right and wrong ways to go about handling a loved one's death? The answer makes all the difference for the future of not only the death care business, but for how every single person should think about the end of life.

It's guidance toward a right way that the hucksters and "disruptors" funded by Silicon Valley and Wall Street have been unable to offer. They're trying feverishly to offer up whatever people *want*, ostensibly paying little attention to the concept of what they *need*.

It's the comfort and confidence that stems from knowing "how to do it right" that the Boomer generation and their children have lost. Through their resistance to institutional knowledge (and institutions themselves) and because of life-altering medical and societal developments in their lifetimes, the Boomers have forgotten how to rebuild the proverbial shrine. As a result, death is less familiar and more disorienting to them than to any generation in history.

It's the idea of a right way, more than anything else, that paralyzes modern funeral professionals. On one hand, they are harassed by public perception and political correctness against asserting that there is such a thing, and on the other, they are taught by their own training and experience that there are not only right ways to approach death, but that there are serious consequences for choosing the wrong ones.

And it was the idea of a right way—and even more specifically, a right way by which funeral professionals lead bereaved families—that Jessica Mitford most viciously attacked when she took aim at the funeral business on behalf of an entire generation.

In her posthumously-published 1998 re-release, *The American Way of Death Revisited*, Mitford railed feverishly against the notion that the "funeral men" whom she so detested could ever be allowed to take on a role of guide or counselor:

> If the public health benefits of embalming are elusive, ten times more so is the role of 'grief therapy,' which is fast becoming a favorite with the funeral men. Trying to pin down the meaning of the phrase is like trying to pick up quicksilver with a fork, for it apparently has no meaning outside funeral trade circles. Although it sounds like a term picked up from the vocabulary of psychology, psychiatrists of whom I inquired were unable to enlighten me because they had never heard of it. "Grief therapy" is most commonly used by funeral men to describe the mental and emotional solace which, they claim, is achieved for the bereaved family as a result of being able to "view" the embalmed and restored deceased. The total absence of authoritative sources on the subject does not stop the undertakers and their spokesmen from

donning the mantle of the psychiatrist when it suits their purposes….Within the trade, [grief therapy] has become a catchall
phrase, its meaning conveniently elastic enough to provide justification for all of its dealings and procedures. Phrases like "therapy
of mourning" and "grief syndrome" trip readily from industry
tongues. The most "therapeutic" funeral, it seems, is the one that
conforms to their pattern, that is to say, the one arranged under
circumstances guaranteeing a maximum profit.[5]

In other words, the people most likely to coach grieving families
toward grief done right are just lying to make a buck.

To be sure, funeral directors must be careful (and haven't always
been in the past) not to conflate self-interest and profit with the personal
needs of a mourning family. I devote Chapters 7 and 10 to that topic
specifically, including some of the industry's past sins, because this is a
crucial aspect of the future. But Mitford's broad attack on funeral directors as selling snake oil and labeling it medicine is simply unfounded.

To accuse someone of impersonating a doctor is to accuse them of a
crime. Funeral professionals need not "don the mantle of the psychiatrist"
to act as experts in an arena in which they work every day. A general contractor with thirty years of experience building houses isn't donning the
mantle of an engineer when he talks about proper framing structure. A
personal trainer isn't donning the mantle of a doctor when she tells you
how to get healthier. And the owner of a local nursery isn't donning the
mantle of a botanist when he advises me on what fertilizer to use. The
notion that morticians have no expertise in grief and no place dispens-
ing advice in it simply because they are not psychiatrists is absurd and
offensive. Funeral professionals spend their entire careers intimately in-
teracting with the grieving and the dead; there is no one who has more expertise on the topic, including the vast majority of psychiatrists. Mitford

here applies a standard that does not exist in any other trade, and uses it to falsely accuse an entire profession of fraud.

Moreover, the fact that "the psychologists of whom [Mitford] inquired were unable to enlighten [her]"[6] is a different issue altogether from whether there is psychological benefit to the advice dispensed by funeral directors. Mitford considers a few personal interactions as proof that "grief therapy"—her shorthand for funeral directors as counselors generally—is an invalid category. For example, she presents an excerpt from her correspondence with Professor Edmund H. Volkart, who writes, "I know of no evidence to support the view that 'public' viewing of an embalmed body is somehow 'therapeutic' to the bereaved."[7]

But the quotation is not the decisive blow that Mitford hoped it would be. Volkart goes on to write, "It would be difficult, if not impossible, to ascertain either its therapeutic or contra-therapeutic effect."[8] In other words, according to Volkart himself, the utility of a public viewing lies beyond that which is measurable and quantifiable by psychiatrists. This would seem to indicate that psychiatry is not a helpful field to answer the question of how to best guide a family to decide, for example, whether or not to conduct a public viewing. But since that would lead to the conclusion that funeral directors *are* the best-qualified professionals available to answer this question, Mitford, of course, dismisses that possibility out of hand.

Mitford's research is simply poor. Psychiatrists and other experts abound who have identified important steps to a healthy grieving process, many of which closely coincide with the advice and services offered by a typical funeral home. Best practices do not vanish with respect to grief simply because antiestablishment voices say they should.

In *Grief Counseling and Grief Therapy*, Dr. J. William Worden of Harvard Medical School outlines "tasks" of grief that must be actively carried out by the bereaved for a successful and healthy healing process.[9] *Psychology Today* writes, "Worden doesn't believe grief is a passive progression of stages that a person is carried through. Rather, Worden empowers mourners to actively engage with four tasks."[10] Worden's thesis bucks the ubiquitous "five stages" conception of grief, arguing that it is indeed harmful to conceive of grief as a passive process through which one inevitably progresses. Instead, to Worden, the bereaved must actively complete "tasks"—a suitably onerous and burdensome term capturing the difficulty and intentionality required to grieve well.

Worden's tasks will be familiar to any funeral director. To mourn, we must (1) Accept the reality of the loss, (2) Experience the pain of grief, (3) Adjust to an environment with the deceased missing, and (4) Find an enduring connection with the deceased while embarking on a new life.[11] The first two are directly correlated with the services of a funeral home immediately following a death, and the latter two are arguably built on a foundation laid by those first steps.

Consider a family who chooses a direct cremation, places Mom's remains on the mantelpiece, and tells one another that she's still "there." By Worden's criteria, they have arguably skipped all four steps. They have not accepted the reality of the loss, having avoided the ceremonies and time for reflection that would have helped them to accept that the loss has actually occurred. For the same reason, they have put off experiencing the pain of grief, choosing instead to pretend that little is different. And as a result, they have forsaken the opportunity to find a meaningful connection to the deceased (instead, they have only a hollow one rooted in denial) and therefore struggle to embark on a new life.

Alternatively, a good funeral director might counsel a family down a different road with different consequences. They are likely to face a sharper, more acute experience in the first days as they go through the rituals of a viewing or a funeral. But this will set a healthy pattern of confronting the loss and pain rather than running from it, and will likely provide helpful catharsis early on. They will likely be advised to lay their mother's remains to rest in a permanent place, so that they are able to return for meaningful visits and reflections at a later date, but also leave Mom (figuratively and literally) behind as they resume their new life.

This is not to say that a viewing, funeral, and burial are the *only* means by which to conduct a healthy grief process, but they are certainly more closely aligned to Worden's criteria than the more passive, recoiling approach that seems so tempting in the first hours of loss.

Liquor ads are rarely built on foundations of solid advice, but a 2015 Johnnie Walker TV commercial is a better mortuary advertisement than most that the funeral business has run for itself.[12] The ad depicts two brothers on a journey together, traveling through numerous obstacles and places over many days. Finally, they reach their destination, and one of the brothers takes out an urn, whose contents he scatters into the sea over a cliff's edge. As he does so, the camera pans and his brother disappears.

While we may wish he had chosen memorialization, this whisky commercial communicates more about proper grief in ninety seconds than volumes written on the subject. The journey took time; the bereaved didn't try to fit in the scattering over his lunch break. He *experienced* the pain, facing both good and bad memories and forcing himself to come to terms with and confront his loss. He made the same journey alone that he had made with his brother, showing his ability to embark on a new life and adjust to a new, different environment. And it's fair to assume that he found a new, enduring connection with the deceased, having laid him to rest in a location significant to his memory.

That's doing it right.

As I've started to talk about "the right way," I've heard a number of colleagues, friends, and even some in the funeral business express frustration with the concept. The most commonly heard concern is that if there's a right way, there must also be a wrong way.

And that's true. There is a wrong way. That's Worden's point. That's not to say that cremation rather than burial, or having a funeral ten days after a death instead of one week after, is "doing it wrong." But, Worden writes, "it is possible for someone to accomplish some of these tasks and not others, and hence have an incomplete adaptation to the loss, just as one might have incomplete healing from a wound."[13] One can hardly argue that an unhealed wound, continuing to fester and cause pain, was a wound handled rightly.

Our culture is on the brink of a pandemic of such incompletely healed wounds. Harris Poll and the Funeral and Memorial Information Council conducted a survey of American adults that found 14 percent of Americans who prefer cremation would choose not to have a funeral or memorial service at all. That's no small number, given the seriousness of what's at stake. That's one out of seven families actively choosing to reject the medicine that would aid and accelerate their grief process. But even more disturbingly, that's one in seven communities that are being denied an invaluable opportunity to actively and healthfully grieve their friend or extended family member.

A friend who works for a mortuary related a story about a gentleman whose golf buddy had passed away. The gentleman was devastated when he called the funeral home to learn that his friend's wife had decided not to hold any funeral or memorial service. He had looked forward to attending his friend's funeral to say goodbye and swap memories with others who knew him. That he was denied this opportunity felt like a betrayal of his friend's memory and a blow to his own grief process.

And tragically, the substantial percentage who intentionally choose against a memorial service are only the tip of the iceberg. Data on memorial services is limited because of the private nature of the events, but we can look to preneed statistics for some interesting indicators. The vast majority of Americans—89 percent—feel a discussion about their end-of-life wishes would be meaningful. But only 69 percent say they would like to pre-arrange their own service. And in practice, only 17 percent have actually made those pre-arrangements.[14] Out of every five families who *say* they will pre-arrange, only one will follow through. When it comes to death, preference and action are very different things.

So, it's reasonable to expect that far more than 14 percent of cremation families will never get around to the memorial they intend to plan on their own. Another study found that 20 percent of American households have cremated remains at home, and fully a third of those (something on the order of 7.7 million households nationwide) don't know what disposition options are available.[15] In other words, people think they'll get around to laying mom to rest, but life and confusion get in the way. Funeral Director Daniel McGraw of Gill Brothers Funeral Chapels in Minneapolis describes a "closet full" of cremated remains that people never came back for. "They say they'll schedule in the spring, and then never do it. Out of sight, out of mind."[16]

Without a funeral home, a family lacks the accountability and guidance to take action. The hardship of confronting the death is a deterrent in itself, and in the context of a culture with less clarity and experience around death and more acceptance toward alternative ways of operating, there are manifold reasons that a family who intends to have a memorial service on their own will never get around to it. These are vulnerable people who are at risk of accidentally harming their own grief process as well as that of the deceased's entire extended community.

Resistance to prescriptive, narrow ideas of a right way is a very different thing from saying there's no such thing as a right (or wrong) way at all. If we fail to accept the reality of the loss, if we avoid the pain of grief, and if we don't adjust to a new environment from which our loved one is absent, then we've done it wrong. That is especially true if we fail to heed the advice of experienced experts and intentionally choose to avoid those difficult steps which aid and encourage healthy grief. This hardly seems controversial. Surely no one could objectively say that they want such an experience for themselves. In fact, it's not kind to look at such a person and say that "she's just doing it her way." It's profoundly unkind and fails to recognize the afflictions of, and remedy for, a very sick patient.

To attend a viewing for a loved one, as anyone who has done so will attest, is a painful thing. But it is impossible to look at the corpse of your loved one while avoiding the reality of the loss; in fact, the pain of doing so is why it is so effective as an aid to the grief process. Confrontation—whether of loss, or of a dilemma, or of a conflict—is well established as a psychologically healthy practice. So much so, in fact, that "avoidance" and "denial" carry heavy negative connotations in both everyday conversations and in discussions of mental health. Under scrutiny, therefore, it's ridiculous to assert that the practices of viewing, ceremony, and memorialization are merely inventions to make money for desperate funeral directors. They are methods of helpfully and healthfully formalizing confrontations that we all need but would rather avoid.

What's important about Worden's criteria is that they steer clear of prescription. There are cases, for instance, where the manner of death makes a viewing particularly difficult or impossible. It would be wrong to say that a viewing is *always* necessary for healthy grief. But what is absolutely necessary is acceptance and experience of the pain of loss. If a family cannot or will not view the body of their loved one for some reason, but they make alternative arrangements to intentionally confront the reality of their loss and experience the pain of saying goodbye, then they are certainly doing death "right"—even if they do so without the aid of a funeral home. But if a family chooses to avoid a viewing or ceremony specifically to avoid pain and confrontation with reality (whether consciously or unconsciously), then we can hardly say that they're grieving well—and we should be under no illusions that pretending they are is to anyone's benefit.

The tools funeral homes offer may not be the only tools available to us, but they are tools that, when available, we would be foolish not to utilize. One might be able to drive in a nail with a brick or the back end of a hatchet in a pinch; a hammer is not the only tool that will do the job. But if you had a hammer and needed to frame out an entire house, you'd be a fool to use a brick. And you would be even more foolish to imagine that you could succeed in building a strong house without ever driving a nail at all.

Worden is hardly alone in his work. Karl E. Jennings, himself an experienced funeral director, outlines similar concepts in his book *When We Must Say Farewell.*[17] Jennings' work—often circulated via the Acute Loss Period model—identifies seven steps through which people must work to beneficially process a loss: hearing, sharing, seeing, gathering, connecting, reflecting, and celebrating.[18] While the components are different, the concept is the same. If deprived of intentional opportunities to recognize that a death has occurred, gather together with the community of the deceased, connect and reflect with others, and celebrate the life that was lived, people have only a truncated, incomplete opportunity to say goodbye.

Dr. Alan D. Wolfelt is a prolific author of more than fifty books about the grief process, and his work has been shared by numerous funeral homes around the country. Wolfelt identifies six "reconciliation needs" or "mourning needs" vital to the bereaved: acknowledge the reality of the death, move toward the pain of the loss, move toward the person who died, develop a new self-identity, search for meaning, and receive ongoing support from others.[19]

The important thing is not the specific components, nor their nuanced differences. What is important is the widely-accepted truth that healthy grief requires certain processes and actions. Whether Worden's four tasks, Wolfelt's six needs, or Jenkins' seven steps, there's no question that healthy grief is aided by certain practices and hindered by their omission.

As though psychology is not enough of an answer, there is remarkable evidence from nature of the importance of intentional mourning.

Shifra Goldenburg with National Geographic has observed and

documented elephants circling and standing near the body of their deceased matriarch for a period of more than two weeks, and even streaming from their temporal glands, an action that indicates heightened levels of stress or emotion.[20] Goldenburg points out that elephants "exhibit these behaviors at dead bodies that they don't exhibit otherwise—certainly an interest in their dead."[21]

The National Wildlife Federation has documented that orca whales, giraffes, elephants, chimpanzees, turtles, baboons, zebras, dolphins, bison, and birds have all demonstrated grief-like behaviors around the bodies of their community members.[22]

A widely circulated 2018 video captured Sadie, a 13-year-old border collie/Dalmatian/shepherd mix, at her owner's side after he died from a sudden heart attack. The dog refused to eat for the ten days between the owner's death and his funeral, but after having an opportunity to see him and spend time with his body at the service, Sadie returned home, ate heartily, and resumed her usual activities.[23]

A stunning photo from 2009 documented sixteen chimpanzees in Cameroon standing behind a fence, lined up to "pay their respects" to Dorothy, a female chimp who had died. As workers carried Dorothy away in a wheelbarrow, the other chimps somberly looked on. [24]

My own firm has conducted research into human death and dying practices around the globe, and I've been struck by the overwhelming ubiquity of ceremony around death. I'm no anthropologist, but I have yet to find evidence of a single human culture without rituals, practices, cultural expectations, and traditions around laying a loved one to rest.

It would seem that within humanity, across history, and even in the context of the animal kingdom more broadly, the modern human preference to silently and unceremoniously dispose of our deceased is unprecedented. The only exceptions have been in extreme circumstances, such as war or famine. In other words, we as a culture are throwing away willingly what others have clung to in all but the most severe of crises.

Funeral directors did not invent the need to recognize communally that a death has occurred. Nor did they make up the idea that people need structured opportunities to recognize and express their grief. It's not funeral directors who are the weird ones. To love someone for years or decades and then avoid public acknowledgement or community when they pass away—and to dispose of their earthly remains in the subtlest and least interruptive manner possible—is not healthy, nor should it be respected as a valid or helpful option. This attempt to avoid the pain of grief is bizarre and unprecedented, not only in human existence, but in nature.

It is important that funeral homes remember this, and that they overcome new obstacles to remain geared to meet families' needs. We've already discussed the differences between mission and model. Mission is the unchanging objective for which we are in business; model is simply the means by which we move toward that mission. It might be that someday there is a better mechanism for every one of the services we offer. But each one of those mechanisms should be aligned with a mission. Wolfelt, Worden, and Jennings all write about *missions*. Families need to "move toward the pain,"[25] or "gather,"[26] or "accept the reality of the loss."[27]

What they don't necessarily need is to attend a viewing or buy a casket. These things might be means to a good end, but doing death "right" is about missions, not models. Every product a funeral home sells should be oriented toward meeting a higher need. Often, morticians end up in the reverse position, treating the need as a rationale to defend the product. But the distinction is important: if you're mission-centric (that is, need-centric), then you're actively seeking opportunities to better meet the needs of the families you serve, even if that means changing up the way you've always done things.

Families need to confront the death, and funeral directors should be committed to helping them do so, whether that means a $10,000 ceremony in your chapel or a $100 consultation about a backyard celebration of life. But if you are model-centric, then you're in the position of defending your GPL to an already skeptical family. The focus shifts from meeting a need to protecting what you're already doing. Families will spot the difference from a mile off.

Here's a useful exercise: take a look at your GPL and challenge yourself to honestly assess the value of each offering to a grieving person. Better yet, take Wolfelt's or Worden's list, so that you have an objective rubric, and ask to what extent each product or service furthers one of those ends, either directly or indirectly. Chances are that most will pass the test, but it's helpful to remind yourself why you sell them in the first place. Others might not, and it might be worth considering whether keeping them around presents any threat to your mission. There's no such thing as a safe decision; we simply weigh one set of risks against others. If you see a revenue opportunity that's only secondary to your mission, your customer might see opportunism that undermines your credibility.

It's worth asking (and has been asked) why we need experts at all. After all, people processed death—and presumably even did so "well" and "right"—for millennia before there were funeral directors.

In his letter to Mitford, Volkart continues:

> The interesting problem to me is why it should be that so many modern Americans seem more incapable of managing loss and/ or grief than other peoples, and why we have such reliance upon specialists. My own hunch is that morbid problems of grief arise only when the relevant laypersons (family members, friends, children, etc.) somehow fail to perform their normal therapeutic roles for the bereaved – or may it be that the bereaved often break down because they simply do not know how to behave under the circumstances?[28]

No doubt most funeral directors have heard these same sentiments expressed by families. "We will get everyone together on our own—why do we need to pay you to do it?" The answer is simple: because there are societal pressures and realities that make that gathering unlikely to happen. A source of outside guidance and accountability is valuable in so many other parts of life—why not in one that is so disorienting and debilitating?

Why, for instance, should we expect that the "relevant laypersons" will gather spontaneously? I've heard preplanning consultants make the poignant observation that the first question people ask when they hear that someone has died is always, "When is the funeral?" People want to know when it's appropriate and acceptable for them to show their support. Especially around death, people are afraid of overstepping and intruding; they need an invitation to do so. Funeral directors don't exist to supplant the friends, family, and community of the bereaved, they exist to facilitate their interaction. If people are unwilling to have a funeral where loved ones can all come together in the memory of the deceased and in support of the survivors, it's unreasonable to expect that they will clearly and extemporaneously understand their roles and how to play them.

Moreover, there is a unique societal situation developing in which Volkart's "relevant laypersons" are indeed less equipped than ever before to "perform their normal therapeutic roles for the bereaved." As funerals have become less common, and as people live longer and spend more of their lives unexposed to death, we see that the same people who a century ago might have known exactly how to support a friend or family member through a loss today have no means by which to gain that education or experience. We are a society that has forgotten how to grieve. In most times and in most places, expecting a community to provide support without any reliance on specialists might have been a reasonable expectation. But today, just as you're unlikely to find someone who knows how to change their own oil or fix their own sink, you're unlikely to find someone with the experience and knowhow to plan their own grief process.

Other complementary specialists, too, have disappeared. Families today are less likely to have a close or trusted member of the clergy who can act as a leader during a loss. With individuals growing more geographically mobile, families are spread out, often leaving no clear family leader with local knowledge and relationships. What was once a shared realm of expertise is increasingly the domain of the funeral director alone.

And options, too, have narrowed. It was once (and in much of the world, still is) acceptable to bury or cremate a loved one yourself, perhaps on the family homestead. But strict regulations prescribing a litany of required steps and actions have simply made death more complicated. There is more to do, and less freedom in which to do it, which further magnifies the need for expert help. If all I had to do was visit the church and dig a grave, I might have some time left to focus on navigating my own grief. But when there are death certificates to be filed, banks and Social Security and Medicare to deal with, life insurance claims to manage, travel arrangements to make, and funeral options to research, I'm left with little bandwidth to spend on researching the psychology of healthy grieving, let alone reflecting and processing it on my own. We'll rely on a real estate agent to save us from missteps in buying a house—why would it be odd to hire a professional to save us from missteps in a process that is even more complicated, far more emotionally taxing, and involves just as much paperwork?

Universally, death rituals address and acknowledge that something significant has occurred. They all allow the living to take part. They all recognize the significance of the deceased. They all happen in different ways, but they happen. In a society that has forgotten how to make them happen, the value and role of an expert should be uncontroversial.

It is important and beneficial that rituals happen. A 2014 Harvard study found that rituals aid in easing the grief process—and notably, that "the benefits of rituals accrued not only to individuals who professed a belief in rituals' effectiveness but also to those who did not."[29] The study concluded that while loss rituals vary widely, "our results suggest a common psychological mechanism underlying their effectiveness: regained feelings of control."[30] Other research has found that absence or avoidance of "mortuary rituals"[31] leads to prolonged grief.[32]

Rituals might involve silence or wailing, worship or drinking, graves or shrines, but they are intentional actions to deal with the death of a loved one. They do not occur passively, and they certainly do not occur by avoidance. The role of a funeral director is rarely to help a family choose between a Baptist or a Buddhist tradition. It is to help them resist the temptation to do nothing at all.

This is important, because that temptation is becoming more prevalent and gaining broader affirmation. It's easier, simpler, and less expensive to not have a funeral. In the short term, it's usually less excruciating. Instinctively, people want to protect themselves from pain, and we know that loss is painful. On top of that, we now have fewer social incentives pushing us toward confrontation and no shortage of excuses pushing us away from it. "Dad wouldn't have wanted a lot of fuss." "He wasn't religious anyway." "It will be hard for everyone to travel this time of year." "We'll do it later." "It's too expensive." "Funeral homes just creep me out—we'll do something when we can get everybody together next summer."

This is the wrong way to grieve: avoidance—and especially socially congratulated avoidance. Postponement. Passivity. Denial. Putting mom in a closet until you can decide what to do with her ashes is not an alternative way to say goodbye; it's choosing not to say goodbye. It is unhealthy, it is going to cause more pain, and it is wrong.

Direct cremation is on the rise. Deaths without any funeral service are at an all-time high. One in five households in America has cremated remains at home.[33] A generation convinced that its parents' institutions and traditions are archaic and unnecessary is poised to make the same sweeping decisions about how to handle death. And it is doing so with less experience and less perspective on the topic than any generation in history.

When, as a young man, I joined my parents and my sister at a mortuary to plan the funeral of my younger brother, my family had decades of experience in funeral service. I had already been to numerous viewings and funerals in my life, and we espoused at every opportunity the value of confronting and actively working through the grief process. Yet in spite of our predispositions, we came within an inch of choosing not to hold a viewing. The reason was simple. We knew how hard it would be. The idea seemed exhausting and violating at a moment when we were already worn down and raw. It was "one more thing" in a week that already had us reeling. We didn't want to deal with it. We didn't want to see the people, or handle the pain, or stand in a room with our son and brother for hours, confronted with the reality of his death.

And yet to this day, I remember that as the night I most fully and completely said goodbye. I remember a line of family and friends wrapping around the building, waiting to console me and support me and honor my family. I remember it as the moment when I first confronted a reality that at the time I would much rather have chosen to avoid.

That is why we need funeral directors who will lead. That is why there is a right way. Not because a viewing in a funeral chapel with hymns playing on the piano is any more correct than a rosary in a Catholic church or a party in an Irish pub. But those aren't the choices we're making. The choices we make are not between doing it our way or doing it some other way—that's just a myth that has denigrated the concept of rightness.

Don't forget which choices are really important. You might spend so much time helping families select an urn or a casket or a chapel that you start to think (like they do) that these are the decisions that define death—and that define a right way of doing death. But the really important choice, which every bereaved has to make at some point, is between confrontation and retreat. The choice between doing it the right, hard way, and doing it the way that seems easier but never helps. The choice between taking the day off to sit by a grave and weep, and going back to work and pretending nothing happened. The choice between wrenching ourselves from our loved one at the graveside with crushing finality, and pretending we can still take them home with us in an urn. The choice between selflessly giving other friends and family a forum in which to work through their pain, and selfishly electing not to have a funeral because it just feels too hard. These are the choices where families are most lost, and where your guidance is the most valuable.

A host of pressures push grieving people toward making the wrong decisions in their most vulnerable moments. Social expectations and prior experience have historically pushed back. But with those gone, there's no force left that would lead an exhausted, disoriented, mourning person to choose the harder, better road. Somebody has to help them.

In twenty-first-century America, there are few social taboos or cultural norms leading us to do the right thing. Our relativistic culture has made tolerance the highest virtue. If you choose not to have a funeral, nobody will breathe a word of disappointment or criticism; if they did, they would be condemned for intolerance and insensitivity. There is simply nobody in our culture today who can look a family in the eye and help them understand the importance of walking the terrible road before them.

Unless you do.

Section 2: The Lies We Tell Ourselves

Chapter 5
Lie #1: We'll Always Have the Body.

In *Good to Great*, Jim Collins made famous what he called the Stockdale Paradox.[1] The concept is named for vice presidential candidate, naval officer, and former Vietnam prisoner of war James Stockdale. To paraphrase both Stockdale and Collins, the idea is that the most surefire path to death in a prison camp is self-deception.

Stockdale was asked, "Who didn't make it out?"

"The optimists," was his surprising answer.

> Oh, they were the ones who said, 'We're going to be out by Christmas.' And Christmas would come, and Christmas would go. Then they'd say, 'We're going to be out by Easter.' And Easter would come, and Easter would go. And then Thanksgiving, and then it would be Christmas again. And they died of a broken heart.[2]

It's not that these heroic prisoners meant to deceive themselves. On the contrary. Keeping a cheery disposition and setting milestones would, on the surface, seem like pretty good strategies for staying sane in the middle of a hellish environment. But in war, as in business, a tenuous grasp on reality can be fatal.

Stockdale's conclusion?

> You must never confuse faith that you will prevail in the end— which you can never afford to lose—with the discipline to

confront the most brutal facts of your current reality, whatever they might be.[3]

Nobody likes to think about brutal facts, but a willingness to look them in the eye and call them what they are, rather than as we would like them to be, is key to survival, whether in a prison camp or in a commoditized business. It's easy, when times are tough, to deceive ourselves and our teams with misplaced hope. Like the truth that Christmas (or three Christmases) might come and go without our release or rescue, the truth that our business has real, fundamental problems can seem like an impossible pill to swallow. But the consequences of self-deception, it turns out, are even worse.

Resolving to face the brutal facts has been important for my own company. My consulting firm has evolved into what it is today largely in response to a chaotic, tumultuous few years for ad agencies—the business model that served us well for our first two decades. But as clients' needs evolved and as agencies were squeezed from every end, many of our peers doubled down on old maxims that they'd used to justify an outdated status quo, running feverishly away from their own brutal reality and insisting that they could survive using a model of misaligned incentives, poor reaction to clients, and myopic focus on industry awards. It only took a few years of mounting pressure to weed out many of the firms that refused to evolve.

"We're slow because we're good." You could say this in virtually any ad agency in America and they'd know what you were talking about. Good creative work is supposed to take a long time, so we could justify spending six months (on an ad our client really needed this quarter) by saying that this was the price of outstanding work. The lie that had protected laziness and complacency came crashing violently down when new competitors arose who were both good and fast. And our clients were able to call our bluff.

Similar self-deceptions abound in other businesses. Lawyers tell themselves that the only way to value their work is via an exorbitant hourly rate, but this incentivizes waste and frivolity at the expense of customers. "There's really no other way to bill in a service business" is a lie; law firms just aren't ready to give up the lavish expectations of their industry. Their model hasn't been toppled yet, but its day is coming, because the pressure of a dissatisfied and frustrated clientele is building.

Financial advisors told themselves for years that the status quo of per-trade commissions and kickbacks from certain investments—both of which put their incentives at odds with those of their clients—were just the way it would always be. New models and approaches pioneered by innovative and client-centric new firms are rapidly putting the old guard out of business.

It may sound obvious, but you can't get a truck out of the mud until you first realize it's stuck. Otherwise, you'll keep spinning your wheels. Work without traction only serves to exacerbate the problem. It can feel like the only option you have is to hit the gas harder, but when you step out to take a look at the situation, you're going to wish that you hadn't kept pressing the pedal.

Let's look a few brutal facts about the funeral industry right in the eye. If you confront them before your competitors do, you won't just have a better defense—you can go on the offensive again.

"We'll Always Have the Body"

I've heard it in almost every mortuary boardroom I've ever visited. It's phrased many different ways: "We'll always have the body," "They'll always need us," "People aren't going to stop dying anytime soon," and my favorite, "Possession is nine-tenths of the law." The word choice varies, but the sentiment is universal: we can't go out of business.

At its best, the statement offers benign reassurance—a cheerful song whistled to oneself while venturing down an ever-darker path. "My family is safe because I chose my profession wisely." "It might have some ups and downs, but death care is a good investment because it's not going anywhere." "Sure, it may not be the glory days anymore, but people are always going to die." "At least we're better off than those guys…"

But at its worst, "We'll always have the body" betrays a brash cynicism. "We don't have to listen to the family, because they're stuck with us."

"We'll always have the body" is the first of three dangerous lies that the funeral business has told itself for decades. And, just like, "We're going to be out by Christmas," it exposes a worrisome refusal to look reality in the eye. Unlike Christmas, we don't know how far off this particular cliff lies. But one way or another, the death care brands that are successful in the future will be those that prepared for a reality in which they do not necessarily have the body.

"We'll always have the body" is a lie for the same reason any lie is: because it's not true. The overwhelming evidence from within and without the industry (we'll address both) proves that assuming any model or position will last forever is a reliably bad bet. And there is mounting evidence on this topic specifically that the winds of time are already blowing hard against the body as any sort of permanent rainy-day fund for the funeral business.

And it must be faced and refuted for the same reason all lies must be: because it is destructive. It is destructive to your relationships with families because it traps you in a position of overconfidence and unresponsiveness. And, as a result, it is destructive to your business because it leaves you irrelevant and unable to meet (or even see) evolving consumer demands.

You're not alone. Not by a long shot. Many, many companies and industries throughout history have assumed that they were too big, too important, or too entrenched to fail. Some have yet to be proven wrong. Others are textbook examples of corporate downfall. Looking to their example can prove instructive in understanding why "we'll always have the body" is such a dangerous belief.

Netflix cofounder Marc Randolph recounts the day in 2000 when he and his colleagues approached Blockbuster with an offer to sell his fledgling online company for $50 million:

> …we were intimidated because Blockbuster was in a much stronger position. Flush with cash from its recent IPO, it wasn't dependent on the good graces of V.C.s to keep it afloat. It wasn't struggling with the scarlet letters ".com." There's nothing like going into a negotiation knowing that the other side holds almost all the cards… This, after all, was a company that had "managed dissatisfaction" as a central pillar of its business model. It knew that most customers didn't enjoy the experience of renting from it, so its goal as a company wasn't so much to make the customer happy as it was to not piss them off so royally that they'd never come back. And there was a lot to piss them off: late fees, crappy selection, dirty stores, poor service—the list went on.[4]

In other words, Blockbuster at the moment of its death looked a lot like American mortuaries today. It was well aware that its customers weren't wild about its business model, but it had them cornered, so it calculated that their dissatisfaction didn't matter. Rental didn't look to be going away, and for years, Blockbuster's customer dissatisfaction had remained uncorrelated to its balance sheet. Blockbuster was now infamously overconfident in its position of established dominance and strength. By the end of the meeting, Randolph observed, Blockbuster's CEO Joe Antioco was trying not to laugh at Netflix.[5]

The story is so poetic because we know how it ends. But that's only because of the perspective of time—in this case, a lot of time. Without that perspective, it wasn't poetic. It wasn't even noteworthy. In fact, it was nineteen years before the story of that meeting would be published in Randolph's book—nineteen years before Randolph was confident enough in the story's end to write down its beginning. It took a decade after that meeting before Blockbuster finally filed for bankruptcy. For ten years the story simply wasn't dramatic at all; it was business as usual for the video rental industry. For a decade, the outcome had yet to be seen.

That's a long time to wait. If you're Blockbuster, that's a long time to double down on the status quo, assuming you made the right call out of a time-tested position of strength. If you're Netflix, that's a long time to grit your teeth and hang in there. At almost any moment along that ten-year timeline, a smart observer might have concluded that the giant had been right to bet on its confidence, and that the little upstart mail-order brand wouldn't last.

Here's the point: in business, you could at any time be blissfully unaware that you're operating within that ten-year gap. It takes a long time for a competitor's idea to take root. It takes even longer for customer dissatisfaction to boil over into outright rebellion. Crippling regulations and Congressional hearings are slower still. The feedback loop for a minor business decision can be tough to discern over quarters of data. The feedback loop for an entire industry's hundred-year business model might have a decades-long lag. But as Netflix taught us, "slow" and "never" are two very different concepts.

There's a well-known astronomical idea that some of the stars we see in the night sky may have already burned out. If a star is seven light-years away, it takes its light seven years to reach the earth. That means we can still see the star, even if it went dark six years ago. In other words, being able to see a star (or a reliable business model) today is not the same thing as being able to rely on its permanence or stability.

We now know that the star by which Blockbuster was navigating had burned out a decade before the company caught on. So, it's not enough to look at the present situation and make a bet on where things stand today. If you're going to make big, bold bets on the permanence of the future, your foresight better be measured in decades, not just years.

That's what's so terrifying—and so dangerous—about "we'll always have the body." It's simply an impossible statement. It's one thing to say, "Today, we have the body," or even, "I bet we'll have the body tomorrow." But to say that no matter what unforeseen regulations, competitors, social changes, and black swans come for the rest of forever, our staple product will never be transformed? This is hubris.

You might argue that I'm taking a flippant remark too seriously. But in my experience, death care professionals believe what they say. It's not a coincidence that a profession that reassures itself of its position's invincibility is also one of the least innovative industries going. That's not an attack; it's simply a fact. If you walked into most modern businesses' counterparts a century ago, they would be unrecognizable. But funeral homes—right down to their décor and service list—have changed very little in a century. That's amazing. This is a business of stability and consistency. The funeral industry values permanence, it protects it, and it advocates for it. That makes it reliable. Unfortunately, it also *assumes* permanence. And that makes it vulnerable.

Because as much as life and death remain the same, some things do change.

Kodak bet that people would always take pictures. So far, they've been right about that. What they got wrong was the assumption that people would always take pictures on 35mm film. The difference between those two ideas was once unappreciated, but it meant everything for a $30 billion company. The funeral industry should take note. There's a big difference between "people will always die" and "we'll always have the body."

Remarkably, Kodak's demise happened during an explosion in photography. Today, people are taking many times more photos than they were a decade ago—it's just that virtually none of them are on film. With the unfolding mortality of the Boomer generation, families will be laying to rest more people than ever before, but it's far from inevitable that they'll be calling on you to help them do so.

The great irony in Kodak's story is that it created the object of its own demise. In the 1970s, Steve Sasson, a Kodak R&D engineer, built a black-and-white prototype of the digital camera. Sasson explained in a *New York Times* interview, "It was filmless photography, so management's reaction was 'that's cute—but don't tell anyone about it.'"[6]

Like Blockbuster, Kodak assumed that its model would last forever—"we'll always have film." Following Sasson's invention, Kodak received 1,000 patents on digital technology but didn't put a digital camera on the market in the following two decades.[7] Its leaders were trying to bury innovation because they saw change as a threat rather than an opportunity (always a dangerous place to be standing). Kodak was the dominant world power in film sales, and film was the cornerstone of its business model, so it's unsurprising that management would have been hesitant to give up the goose that laid the golden egg.

In 1994, Apple introduced the Quicktake 100, an early digital camera.[8] It was marketed as an Apple product… but manufactured by Kodak. The film titan was so committed to its foundational revenue stream that it willingly sacrificed brand capital to competitors in new spaces, even when it had the technology, manufacturing expertise, and history to stand out as a leader. Its commitment to the status quo business model was fatal, not just because of head-in-the-sand passivity, but because of active decisions to distance itself from new models and approaches.

Kodak and Blockbuster provide valuable perspective and a warning to funeral homes to not take the same path, lest they share the same fate. But we need look no further than funeral service itself for evidence that the status quo is less than permanent; in fact, the certainty of this business is already on shaky ground.

"We'll always have the body" is essentially the assumption that nobody else will ever handle disposition, so there's at least one revenue stream not in jeopardy. And that assumption rests heavily on government regulation. After all, it seems a good bet that you'll always be in business if people will always die and it's illegal to take them anywhere else. But those regulations may not be as iron-clad as they seem.

The Tennessee state legislature considered a bill in 2020 to deregulate funeral directors along with a long list of other professions, including tattoo artists.[9] Connecticut has considered deregulating funeral homes as a cost-saving measure.[10] So has Wisconsin.[11] Arizona and Pennsylvania have enacted universal recognition bills, which lower the regulatory barrier by allowing the state to grant broad, inclusive reciprocity to funeral licensure offered by other states.[12] Mississippi and Ohio have considered similar legislation.[13] A group of Catholic monks in Louisiana won a long legal battle in that state for the right to offer some death care services.[14] Colorado has no licensing requirements for funeral directors and few for the death business generally.[15]

This trend toward removing morticians' protective barrier is indicative of a mounting (and valid) critique. Tanya Marsh, a law professor at Wake Forest University who specializes in funeral and cemetery law, argues that "embalming is the centerpiece of the entire occupational licensing structure for the funeral services industry," but with cremation on the rise, this focus is anachronistic.[16] She has publicly advocated for broad deregulation, as the regulation that exists (like mandated casket selection rooms) is increasingly irrelevant to modern practice.

Today, most funeral homes can continue to ply their trade without fear of external competition, thanks to regulatory protections. But that protection is increasingly fragile, and it's certainly a brittle foundation upon which to build your future.

And other business models are not unprecedented, even in the West. England uses a system of public crematoria, effectively making disposition possible without any mortuary (or for-profit company) involved at all. With public preferences in the U.S. shifting increasingly toward nationalization and publicization of traditionally for-profit services, it's not difficult to imagine this model coming to America. In one focus group study my firm conducted, a participant discussing the funeral business commented that "it's weird that it's profitized," to hearty agreement from the other contributors.[17] Before we assume that "we'll always have the body," we should consider the likelihood that other alternatives may yet upend the status quo as they have other categories.

Such alternatives are more apt to gain public support as public frustration with the business mounts. This is the vicious cycle around "we'll always have the body." The more the industry says it, the more likely it is to give its customers reason to seek alternatives. The more funeral service reassures itself that the category is "safe," the more likely its overthrow becomes.

Resting on its laurels leads any company to its downfall. BlackBerry was a shorter-lived example of this principle than the more protracted collapses of Blockbuster and Kodak, but no less telling. For a brief moment in the early 2000s, BlackBerry was synonymous with smartphones. For many professionals today, BlackBerry represented their first experience with email from a mobile device. In 2009, *Fortune* named BlackBerry the fastest growing company in the world. But within just a few years, the company's stock price collapsed by a sickening 90 percent. [18]

Writing for *Time*, journalist Sam Gustin observed key mistakes in BlackBerry's strategy:

> BlackBerry's failure to keep up with Apple and Google was a consequence of errors in its strategy and vision. First, after growing to dominate the corporate market, BlackBerry failed to anticipate that consumers—not business customers—would drive the smartphone revolution. Second, BlackBerry was blindsided by the emergence of the "app economy," which drove massive adoption of iPhone and Android-based devices. Third, BlackBerry failed to realize that smartphones would evolve beyond mere communication devices to become full-fledged mobile entertainment hubs. [19]

In other words, BlackBerry assumed things would stay the same, and it did so on all levels. In terms of promotion, it failed to prepare for different sales models, such as Apple's consumer-focused approach. In product design, it failed to plan against the rapid evolution and customization that Apple built into its product. In optimization, it failed to anticipate personal applications of its business-centric product. Blackberry's failures all fall under the header of the assumption of permanence. This is an important lesson for funeral homes: you can't be agile in reacting to your customers' needs at the micro level while you're rigid in defining your business model at the macro level. You're either assuming a fluid, responsive, customer-centric future, or you're not.

BlackBerry's leaders weren't fools. They had reason to be confident. Massive government and corporate contracts drove the company's early success as it dominated market share on Wall Street and Capitol Hill. For a few shining years, the company was synonymous with corporate communication, a symbol of upward mobility, sophisticated white-collar employment, and the importance that comes with connectedness. When I was working as a congressional aide in 2010, my colleagues swore that we'd never switch to mobile devices that didn't include a physical keyboard. Like BlackBerry, we just didn't see what was coming.

Selling a million BlackBerrys in a single federal contract is an appealing (and lucrative) approach. But it's nothing compared to putting an iPhone in the pocket of every individual in America. Writes Gustin, "BlackBerry saw its devices as fancy, e-mail-enabled mobile phones. Apple and Google envisioned powerful mobile computers..."[20] You might argue that BlackBerry built its product for the wrong target: the procurement officers who wanted a business machine. Instead, its competitors made something *users* liked. The distinction made all the difference.

BlackBerry assumed that it would always have the smartphone market. When that ground was challenged, it assumed it would always have corporate America. For a brief period near the end of its run, while government contracts had yet to phase out, it assumed that it would always have federal employees. Today, it has none of these. The danger of the "we'll always have…" mindset isn't just false assurance—it's restrictive permanence. In 2009, the Capitol Hill contract was a sign of burgeoning strength in a virgin category. In 2013, the same contract had become an albatross, a sign of clumsy bureaucratic stodginess amidst an increasingly individualistic and agile market.

Blockbuster's "we'll always have…" mindset was similar. Having millions of slightly annoyed customers was a tremendous asset in a market with no alternatives. But the moment Netflix became a viable option, the minor annoyance that had been irrelevant a few years prior became a gaping weakness that dozens of digital competitors were delighted to exploit.

Like a medieval castle perched safely on a hill, an entrenched market position has its advantages. But when you need to maneuver and go on the offensive, heavy and immovable edifices become liabilities in an instant.

In other words, you might not even *want* to always have the body. Today, it sounds like a reassuring asset—if not an ace, then at least a king up your sleeve. But tomorrow, it could become a liability. If other products and services around death continue to grow in prominence, the body will likely continue to wane in value. Cremation has already opened the door to ceremony without the deceased. Cenotaphs, scatterings, and DIY markers have divorced the mortal remains from memorialization as well. All trends would indicate that the body—already a commoditized, low-margin, race-to-the-bottom portion of the business—is only going to become less valued and less profitable as a revenue source. And that doesn't even consider the very likely possibility of a new technology, new legislation, new biomedical concerns, or new social patterns that could displace the relevance of the body altogether.

During the COVID-19 outbreak that began in 2020, many funeral homes around the country were severely impacted by a perfect storm of disastrous conditions. Health concerns left many mortuaries unable to keep up with demand as funeral directors refused to handle COVID cases, an amplification of a broader labor shortage in the business. Mortality rates spiked, meaning that case count was up higher than ever before. But social distancing and isolation requirements meant that averages declined drastically—not for want of bodies, but for want of ancillary business. In an interview with *Forbes,* Tom Ryan of SCI explained that "our ability to get in front of the consumer is limited." *Forbes* was not so delicate in its commentary: "the pandemic severely limits SCI's ability to upsell the bereaved."[21]

No matter how you phrase it, the pandemic provided insight into another danger of assuming we'll always have the body. The body alone just might not be enough. The funeral business today is based on a revenue model that extends far beyond disposition alone. Even low-cost and direct cremation outfits derive a significant portion of their revenue from product and merchandise sales. To exist solely as a disposition company is a bleak and unprofitable reality. Unless that's the business you want to go into, then the idea that disposition is an unchanging need is hardly reassuring.

We've already tried it, thanks to COVID. Many of your colleagues across the country had an increased demand for disposition services—and practically nothing else. It was one of the most difficult periods in the history of those firms, both financially and psychologically. Even if we always have the body, having the body alone is not a future most owners really want to have. Both families and providers need something more. It's not helpful to have an infinite supply of food if you don't have any drinkable water.

The death business has seen this kind of sudden disruption on a considerable scale before, so it's all the more surprising that it continues to cling to assumptions about what will not change. The industry has already been served hard lessons in how much more *does* change than it would have previously imagined. It's reminiscent of Stockdale's optimists, and just as tragic. We're in tough conditions, beaten, starving, fighting for our lives, and remembering how much better it was in the old days when we were free. And yet we will not let go of the fatal and unfounded belief that we'll miraculously be rescued by Christmas.

In 1960, it would have seemed reasonable to say, "We'll always have burial." The Catholic church had an official ban on cremation, and American cultural taboo imposed an unofficial one. But today, burial is not only not guaranteed, it's not even preferred.

Caskets reflected a similar evolution. Historically, funeral homes lobbied for requirements dictating the sizes and options available in a casket selection room—details that many state thanatopractice boards still regulate. Once upon a time, these regulations protected funeral homes from upstarts who lacked the capital to invest in both a large space and a wide array of sample caskets to display. If only the big guys could play, then the little guys posed no threat. It was protectionism, plain and simple, and it worked for a long time.

Today, as cremation rates have skyrocketed and caskets offer a plummeting share of ROI, those same legally-mandated casket selection rooms have been transformed into liabilities. I've stood in casket selection rooms from coast to coast and had discussions with owners about the intricacies of whether a particular state allows "sectional displays" or whether they are still required to exhibit full caskets. There is even a lexicon of colorful terminology around this question specifically. Partial casket displays, when they're allowed, are referred to as "corners," "sections," and even, euphemistically, "butts and cheeks." It's all couched in terms of "what we can get away with" and when (or whether) the state will "let us switch."

What a terribly odd conversation. The industry as a whole assumes it will always have the body. Once, it assumed it would always have an intact, embalmed, uncremated body. And it invested heavily and successfully in protecting that particular turf. But the securely built fort has been transformed into a prison, leaving its residents unable to shift to more important ground. You can't repurpose this space (physically or figuratively) into something more relevant, because the industry got the law it asked for.

Funeral service was wrong about cremation. It was wrong about the permanence of caskets and embalming. But it can't imagine that it is wrong about the body itself. On reflection, it's difficult to think of any thriving, nimble, customer-oriented business having conversations about such narrow and arcane details of product displays.

And that's the most important reason why "we'll always have the body" is such a destructive statement. It separates the funeral director from the family's most intimate needs.

Think of a brand with which you identify—perhaps your favorite clothing brand or a restaurant you frequent. Chances are you like the feeling of being courted by that company. If a maître d' smiles and welcomes you by name, or if you get special discounts and shopping privileges, you know that they're working for you. This is why those gestures are such effective marketing tools; a business transaction is improved by efforts to customize and tailor the experience to a specific customer. Amazon lacks the personal touch, but part of its genius as a retailer is its incredibly sophisticated approach to constantly recommending products specifically for each user. Amazon doesn't take me for granted; it's constantly on the lookout for new products I might enjoy.

For years, I bought my suits from a particular local tailor (I am, after all, a funeral director's son). He was so good at what he did that I considered it a personal loss when he retired. But before he did, he taught me a vital lesson on the importance of hustle in business. He would always call me to let me know when the sales were coming so I could come in a week early and make some selections before the rush. Then he'd set them aside and ring me up once the sale was on. It was a gratifying gesture, and one that kept me as a loyal customer. It was the opposite of taking me for granted. He never thought, despite our history and a strong professional relationship, that "I'll always have Eric." Instead, he continued to work for my business, and went above and beyond to repeatedly earn it.

The funeral business instinctively understands this basic customer service concept. In fact, in many aspects of the business, practitioners work desperately to be "all things to all people," earning families' business through an intense and laudable dedication to personal service and customization. But this is only *within* the existing model, which is growing worryingly irrelevant.

Imagine trying to order something off-menu at your favorite high-end restaurant, only to overhear the waiter scoff, "We don't have to make any exceptions for him—we'll always have him as a customer anyway." Or if your favorite clothing brand announced that it would not be carrying a new line you'd hoped for because it would always have your business. I'm certain that "we'll always have the body" is a phrase its adherents would never utter in front of a family, which might be a clue that they shouldn't think it at all.

If funeral directors assume they'll always have the body, they undermine their ability to serve their customers the way they want to in two very important ways. First, when they presume that they already know the means by which they can best serve families, they stop looking for ways to serve them better. It's like a chef assuming there's no need to create new recipes, or a fashion brand refusing to put out a new spring line. Customers are served best—and courted best—when businesses are constantly looking for new ways to serve them. In "we'll always have the body," death care has planted its flag on a rather poor hill, and stopped looking for better ones.

Second, this leads the business to assume it can't lose its customers at all, which is even more dangerous. There is a healthy and productive pressure in business that comes from the fear of losing a customer. It forces brands to stay relevant, keep working hard, and keep trying. Customers don't like being thought of as a sure thing.

"Never stop dating your spouse" is a sound, if clichéd, piece of marriage advice. The idea is to never let complacency take root. In saying, "We'll always have the body," today's funeral industry has stopped dating its customers. As a result, the relationship is withering and the customers will eventually look elsewhere. Blockbuster, Kodak, and BlackBerry all stopped dating their customers, and the rest is history.

So did taxi companies. It's a well-worn case study, and most of the attempts to create "the Uber of Funeral Service" have fallen flat, like most attempts to create the Uber of anything. But the analogy is so fitting here that I would be remiss to exclude it.

The Washington Post once called taxi medallions "the best investment in America."[22] In an arrangement reminiscent of casket selection room mandates, a taxi medallion represented a pact. "In exchange for all of this regulation," wrote the *Post*, "taxis have for decades held a government-backed monopoly."[23]

As in funeral care, taxi regulation has always been extensive; there are laws mandating colors, lights, displays, stickers, fees, payment methods, and safety. There are a million things for owners and drivers to worry about besides the customer. So, reasons abound why a taxi ride would be an unpleasant one. It's not a business with a lot of room to maneuver; both the business and the model are dictated by municipal statute. But cab companies have nobody but themselves to blame for this; as in funeral care, the industry leaders willingly sought out regulatory walls to keep out the competition.

But like Blockbuster's marginally unhappy customer, taxi riders were, for decades, frustrated but tolerant. In fact, "We'll always have the medallion," could have been the industry motto. The *Post* observed that medallions historically outperformed the S&P 500 as an investment. At their peak in New York, medallions exceeded a million dollars in value. They commanded three quarters of a million dollars in Boston, nearly half a million in Philadelphia, and $300,000 in Miami. Over a five-year stretch in the early 2000s in Chicago, their value doubled.[24]

All of this led those who owned taxi medallions to fall asleep at the wheel. They sat on multimillion-dollar investments that could always be sold off in a pinch but seemed guaranteed to appreciate indefinitely. Demand was steady. Competition was nonexistent. Sure, the cabs were gross, the drivers surly, and the rides disagreeable, but why change? We'll always have the medallion—nobody can take away our business. In fact, the government will ensure that under force of law.

The unpleasantness of your average cab ride was not unrelated to the high barriers of entry around the industry; it was because of them. There's nothing (as we've learned since) about a hired ride in a stranger's car that is inherently miserable. It can be a clean, enjoyable experience. But it's only made so by the constructive forces of competition, which is why antitrust laws are at least conceptually uncontroversial. At no point on the political spectrum will you hear a politician openly advocating for fewer, more heavily protected businesses. Monopolies, real or imagined, aren't good for anybody. Competition is tough, but it's good for everybody, because it ignites the fire needed to motivate invention, service, and improvement. Without it, there is only stagnancy.

But when customers are cornered by a monopoly and poorly served by the products it generates, it's difficult to overstate the sheer force of the resulting reaction. Uber has battled lawsuits, regulations, fines, and blowback from municipal and taxi industry forces since its inception.[25] It has been estimated that the company's legal and lobbying efforts have reached into the hundreds of millions of dollars.[26] In the early days of rideshare services, Uber and Lyft operated illegally, in defiance of local statutes, in numerous municipalities.[27] Despite all of this resistance and the incredible costs of facing it, Uber and its investors have calculated that the payoff from serving anti-cab customers will be greater still.

All of this underscores the sheer frustration consumers continue to have with the status quo of taxi companies. If taxis were anywhere close to an acceptable alternative to Uber, then none of this investment and risk would be remotely warranted. But the pent-up demand was so great that when it was finally given an outlet, medallion values—representative of the relevance and value of the companies that owned them—evaporated almost overnight.

Medallion owners were never incentivized to get in the back of the cab. But if they had, they could easily have listed all of the ways in which their product was misaligned with what their customers wanted. It's not that the industry didn't realize that customer satisfaction was nonexistent—like Blockbuster, its philosophy was one of "managed dissatisfaction." Cab companies knew the misalignment was there. They just told themselves it didn't matter.

That's what frightens me most about funeral service today. As a whole, I believe deeply that this is a good and valuable profession. But the specific ways in which the services provided are at odds with what customers really want and need are numerous. The sales process is outdated. The incentives are misaligned with customers' interests. The stylings, jargon, and practices are archaic. The training and licensing focus on increasingly irrelevant products and services. Customer approval, relative to other businesses and products, is abysmal. It's no secret that the death business is on its way out.

But so are we. So are all people. Funeral directors should know that better than anyone. Decline itself isn't the problem—all of us, and all of our businesses, are in a constant state of decay. If we recognize that, we can actively manage against it, like a cutter ship tacking into the wind. But if, like Stockdale's campmates, we pretend that we're not dying, that our business model need never be adjusted, or that our sails need never be trimmed, then there is no saving us. Like Blockbuster, or Kodak, or BlackBerry, our fate is already decided—and by our own doing.

Chapter 6
Lie #2: We're All Things to All People.

"Remember, above all, that many funeral homes have a 'no-walk' policy, which means simply that if and when you start to walk out, the price will come down, down, down until a level acceptable to you is reached."[1]

—Jessica Mitford, *The American Way of Death Revisited*

What is your favorite brand?

Perhaps a musician you love to listen to (yes, artists are brands). Or a social commentator you follow on Twitter. A clothing brand that you love to wear. A car you wish you owned. Or a reliable product you can depend on.

Now imagine you're in that brand's boardroom. The executives are deciding that they need to take a new course. "We need to be all things to all people," they say. "It's no longer enough to just focus on our traditional audience. We need everybody."

Hopefully, you would be disappointed—what made you love the brand was that it loves *you*. Not everybody. Just you, and people like you. Whether it's the style, the sound, the fit, the design, or the application, there's something about this particular brand that is *yours*. If they made it for everybody, then it would be less yours. It would be less precious to you. There's no such thing as strong general appeal; breadth and focus are opposites. You know instinctively that trying to make everybody happy is going to make the brand worse at making *you* happy.

That's why good brands are focused brands. It's as simple as that. You can't have everything. The narrower your target audience, the greater you can make the intensity of your brand's appeal.

The opposite is also true. That's why we can all name examples of "sellouts"—brands we once admired that lost a little of their appeal once they went mainstream. Not many people are aware that Abercrombie & Fitch was once an elite sporting-goods brand for clients like Ernest Hemingway and Teddy Roosevelt, but it's safe to say that core audience would miss the good old days if it saw the brand today. *Star Wars* had a devoted fan following when the first film was released in the '70s, but fans have complained since *Return of the Jedi* about attempts to widen the appeal of the franchise by including content aimed at children and more general audiences. When Harley Davidson looked to expand its target audience via the Buell brand, a stripped-down bike marketed at Gen-Xers, the backlash from Harley's traditional Boomer devotees was so strong that Harley killed the Buell line after just six years.

Brands that try to win everybody often lose everybody. But brands that go narrow can, paradoxically, expand their audience.

Scotch whisky brand Laphroaig ran an ad campaign centered on its powerful flavor profile, cementing its reputation as a Scotch-drinker's Scotch. The brand has proudly advertised a comparison of the Laphroaig experience to "eating some burnt barbeque driftwood,"[2] a statement that it's "like drinking from a wooden medicine cabinet while it's on fire,"[3] and a claim that it tastes like "burnt Harley engine oil."[4] The campaign has contributed to the brand's success; it singlehandedly dominates the market for whiskies of its style and profile, gulping nearly half of global market share in its niche.[5]

If Laphroaig tried to appeal to everyone by downplaying its polarizing flavors, it would likely be a hit with no one. But Laphroaig's audience takes special pride in enjoying something that the rest of the world considers downright nasty. By emphasizing that fact instead of ignoring it, Laphroaig earns special credibility among its target market. To those people, it defines itself as *the* strong, smoky Scotch brand rather than one among many. They could order another brand—perhaps even one they really enjoy more—or they could order one that gives them insider status as an elite, serious Scotch drinker.[6] Laphroaig narrows its target audience, but in doing so it also narrows its competitive set and increases its strength of appeal.

It's a tried-and-true strategy. Google once ran a billboard campaign that featured no logo, no website, and no contact information—just a math problem that, if solved, would lead the target to a job application.[7] Google, like Laphroaig, appealed to its target precisely by driving away everyone else. But by doing so, it won the attention and admiration of the few with the training and brains to get in on the joke.[8]

Amazon, which sells practically everything, might be the closest example to a brand that has truly delivered on the concept of being all things to all people. But even Amazon works hard to focus, using some of the most sophisticated marketing technology in the world to present hyper-customized options. Your Amazon dashboard looks nothing like mine, which is to say that Amazon is something entirely different to you than it is to me. Even with unprecedented breadth, Amazon maintains remarkable focus and specificity. That matters, because few businesses have the resources or sophistication to make themselves into such a chameleon. It's one of Amazon's greatest competitive advantages.

Even Walmart, another broad-base brand, is more narrowly focused than it looks. Brand targeting, after all, is about who you seek, not about who you'll take. Few companies are going to turn away a paying customer at the door; that's just the hyperbolic mental image that trips us up when we think about focusing. Most people have shopped at Walmart at one point or another, but the brand's core customer is someone who lives paycheck to paycheck. Walmart has defined and built itself around that target audience in some very specific ways.

For example, you can buy the exact same products at both Walmart and Target, but Walmart shoppers report traveling less and preferring more conservative political candidates than Target shoppers.[9] In other words, Walmart's core customer is not just "somebody who needs groceries and home supplies." Both Walmart and Target know who they're after, and they tailor customer experiences accordingly.

The most successful brands know who their target audiences are—and who they aren't. This is a foundational principle of good marketing (and good business) that has been forgotten in mortuary boardrooms, beaten back by the misguided idea that being "all things to all people" is a good thing—or at least a necessary one.

The rationale is not unreasonable. Death care professionals readily explain that because the industry by definition has a fixed demand (though we've all heard the jokes about drumming up extra business), the stakes are higher with every case. You can't grow the pie the same way Apple can by injecting demand for a new product or a new upgrade; all you can do is focus on getting your slice of it. And when that slice is threatened, you'll make the concessions you believe you need to keep it.

This has led to both explicit and implicit decisions to rely on what Mitford calls "no-walk policies." Many funeral homes have such policies in practice, even if not in principle. Any company should have a list of the types of products and services within its category for which it is best suited, and a corresponding list of the products and services for which it is ill-suited or will not provide. Ideally, these lists should be clearly articulated and printed, but even mental lists are helpful. Most funeral homes have no such list. If it's within the realm of death care and is requested by a family, they would find a way to get it done.

Not only that, but most funeral directors reject even the concept of such a list. It's a badge of honor to be all things to all people. It's part of the calling—proof that we're here to serve, standing at the ready to provide whatever the family desires.

But none of it is true. You don't have to be all things to all people. Nor, really, can you be. Higher case count is not the only way to success as a brand. Quite the opposite; in other commoditized industries, where demand is more fixed, the most successful brands are those who are the most disciplined and most focused on their target audience and brand identity—never those who are the most appeasing. What is often seen within the calling as a badge of honor may in fact be costing both you and your employees the credibility and confidence you need to succeed.

Cases

"We have to capture one hundred percent of the leads we get, because we only get so many."

That sounds like solid logic. There is undeniably something unique about the business of death in that regard; I don't know of another industry where state agencies reliably publish documentation of the total units sold in a month, such that a company can readily calculate not only its own market share but that of its competitors. Many mortuaries succumb to the temptation to obsess over these figures, counting gains or losses of just a few cases a month as the best data available on their success or failure as a business.

The context was a bit different, but the U.S. military once also counted bodies as a flawed means of gauging success. During the Vietnam War, then-Secretary of Defense Robert McNamara used body count as evidence that the U.S. was winning the war, because more North Vietnamese soldiers than American soldiers were dying.[10] But it soon became obvious that the numbers, precise though they were, didn't tell the whole story. America was losing the war, even if it was winning the body count.

Consultant Tim Williams uses the Vietnam example to explain that metrics aren't everything and in fact that the wrong metrics can provide a false sense of security.[11] Like McNamara, the funeral business could be counting the wrong thing. Williams quotes W. Bruce Cameron in observing, "Not everything that counts can be counted, and not everything that can be counted counts."[12]

Body counts shouldn't be the primary metric of success for your firm either. A competitor might have a much larger case count than your shop, but he might be sacrificing margins—or even going into debt—to get it. Meanwhile, another competitor who seems small by caseload might be more profitable, more successful, and happier. Unless your objective is to handle the body of every person who dies in your city (and it shouldn't be—this would be as arbitrary as opening a grocery store just to make sure you're the only person who sells asparagus), then case count should only be a means to some other end, not the end itself.

Consider two scenarios: In Scenario A, you can grow case volume by ten percent next year, but to make it work you spend most of the additional revenue on new hires, and you have to work more yourself. In Scenario B, case volume remains flat, but you fine-tune your business such that you're more profitable, you're happier, you have more time with your family, and families say they're better served. Which would you prefer?

The nice thing about math in business is that there's always more than one variable. We can choose where we focus. The prevailing industry wisdom tells you to maximize case counts (which implies a need to do whatever it takes to get those cases). But that doesn't mean volume is the only path to success. If you need to hit a certain revenue target, you can do that by converting a given percentage of leads. Or, you can get more leads and convert a smaller percentage of them. Better still is when you can do both—more leads and a higher conversion rate. Or you can get fewer leads, convert fewer still, but cut costs and increase averages so that profit still grows. The point is that there are numerous ways to hit goals without sacrificing your brand identity.

Marketing is a good place to start. Most funeral homes operate within a sales paradigm rather than a marketing paradigm. The history of funeral homes is sales: relational, communal, face-to-face. You market your business by becoming a member of the Rotary club, sponsoring the Little League team, and taking out ads in church bulletins. Even those ads might have your face on them, because they're treated as a proxy for the face-to-face world in which you're most comfortable. The real work happens at the time of need, when an associate is sitting across the table from a family making arrangements.

Funeral service has adopted, intentionally or not, a sales model built to respond to fixed demand—specifically, to maximize close rates of a fixed percentage of leads out of a fixed pool of cases. There's nothing wrong with this approach, but it is reactive. You're in a position of re-sponding to whoever walks in the door, rather than proactively setting their expectations (and filtering out ill-fitting customers) in advance.

The alternative is to tell customers—loudly—what you're here for. The workwear brand Carhartt once ran a successful ad with the headline "Designed where function meets fashion—then punches it in the face."[13] Carhartt's heavy canvas jackets are never going to be the choice of the style-savvy, but it would be tempting to cast a wide net to attract both the style-conscious and the function-conscious. "Looks great and performs even better." But by focusing on what it's uniquely good at and who its core customer uniquely is, the brand builds credibility among those who also proudly see themselves as too tough, hard-working, and function-focused to care about the latest trends. In other words, Carhartt recognizes it can't be all things to all people and gets a lot further by openly admitting its shortcomings than it would by trying to ignore or make excuses for them. Like a general who strengthens a key position by sacrificing unimportant ground, brands that know exactly what their target audiences are looking for are able to appeal to them with laser focus, giving up the weak points that just don't matter.

When my firm is working in a new market, we usually conduct a competitive analysis of the other mortuaries in the area, and when we do, it's not unusual to discover that a competitor has a website with the same images and some of the same copy. Often *exactly* the same. This happens when two competitors use the same website vendor, and neither competitor nor the vendor takes the initiative to ensure differentiation. So, your families all see the same thing, and they figure one funeral home is as good as another.

But if freed from the trap of the generic, marketing could go from dim glow to powerful beacon. Even if it feels like you're cornered, you're not. You have options. You don't have to close every sale—it's far better to attract the *right* sales. A family choosing another firm that's a better fit might be the best thing for both of you.

Commodities

In many ways, the arguments around "all things to all people" are admissions of commoditization. There's no way to goose demand; you operate in a cutthroat, red-ocean market, and customers are price-shopping you. So there's no choice but to act as a commodity, reacting in the moment to the price pressures and demands of every client, selling until you get your hand slapped and then retreating so as not to upset (and heaven forbid, lose) the family.

But funeral homes actually tend to go to market using the *opposite* of proven strategy for commoditized industries. If you have a commodity to sell (think toothpaste), are you going to use an army of expensive salesmen to convey the benefits of your brand to every customer? Or would you use broad channels to cast a wide net, spending your efforts on planting seeds long before your customer is standing in the drugstore aisle?

Procter & Gamble is the undisputed master of commodity marketing. The company sells nothing but commodities. Laundry detergent and bar soap are hardly growth categories or big disruptors. Razors aren't an area that has seen much innovation in the last few decades, and people won't stand in line for hours to get the new upgrade on the latest deodorant brand. Margins are low. Competition is fierce. Pennies matter. Demand is fixed.

In Chapter 3, we discussed the Disruption Cycle, my firm's take on how to classify industries based on their market situation. Most funeral home owners tend to say they're in the "maturation" or "saturation" phases of business—the parts of the cycle where customer perceived value is still relatively high, and where the race to the bottom hasn't yet sunk in. Still, it's tough to deny that funeral service has a lot in common with brands in the later commoditization phase, where competition is fierce, margins are dwindling, the disruption that invented the industry feels like a distant memory, and true differentiation between products is rare.

Unlike funeral homes, leaders in the commodity business invest seriously in marketing. In any year, Procter & Gamble is likely to spend north of $7 billion on advertising.[14] That's billion with a B—in an industry where products are compared in terms of cents per ounce and where demand is fixed almost as permanently as it is in the funeral business. By dominating everything from the Super Bowl to digital advertising, P&G brands like Tide and Old Spice guarantee that their products outperform the competition, both on store shelves and in margin performance.

P&G's marketing makes sure that customers value its brands more highly when it's time to make a purchase decision. All things being equal, a P&G brand will command a higher price, meaning P&G makes a higher margin, such that the investment pays for itself. But there's also a volume benefit; P&G tips the decision scales in its favor so that customers are not just more willing to spend more on its products—they're more likely to select its products. This means that P&G sales perform better than the competitors, all else being equal, *and* that P&G margins are wider.

What P&G does *not* do is cut corners on advertising. Nor does it beg customers to stick around with discount plays. While these are common strategies, especially for commodities (generic brands will pick up a few dollars by doing both), it's what you do when you're playing to not lose—not when you're playing to win. Walmart's Great Value brand generates some revenue for the retailer, but it will never touch Tide in terms of either market share or net income.

In the same way, the pressures forcing the death business into commoditization should be pushing it toward *greater* investment in branding and *greater* differentiation in terms of targeting and focus—exactly the opposite of what is happening today.

Confidence

At this point, you might be thinking that your firm has more differences from Procter and Gamble than it has similarities. After all, a funeral home is not selling products that customers pick off of a shelf. And to be fair, plenty of concierge brands win points (and remain differentiated) by doing whatever people ask them to. Not many hotels—certainly none of the caliber you would aspire to emulate—would refuse to perform a special request for a guest. To be sure, the "service" aspect of funeral service must be respected. It's the heart of the business, and it is absolutely unlike a tube of toothpaste.

But like so much else in this line of work, heart matters. To act out of a position of confidence as a premier brand is entirely different than to act out of desperation and fear. A few hotels are "all things," but they are only so to "some people" (and a very select group of people at that). If I ask for a framed portrait of my favorite celebrity at the Ritz Carlton, the staff will accommodate me to the point that they become famous for their willingness to go above and beyond. But if I ask for the same thing at a Motel 6, I'll be laughed out of the lobby. No hotel with a $55 nightly rate is going to make any pretense of being "all things" for its guests. You can be one or two things to all people, or you can be all things to a select few. You cannot be both.

The difference is confidence, and it's both the reason and the result in this case. A confident brand is one that is able to be "all things" without coming off as pandering or sycophantic. A single night at a Ritz Carlton could cost four figures—they're not desperate for my business, and their price tag says so. Because Ritz Carlton is a confident brand, it therefore makes disciplined decisions in its pricing, offerings, and marketing, going after only those able to afford their premium rate.

But the opposite is also true. Ritz Carlton is focused because it is confident. And because Ritz Carlton makes disciplined brand decisions, it is able to operate with confidence. Imagine the confidence needed to set a dress code for an elite customer. Requiring a gentleman to put on a jacket for dinner is not something most brands can get away with, which is why only a tiny fraction of restaurants still do so. But if you've carefully and diligently refined your target audience, you know ahead of time that your customer is someone who will not only respect and appreciate those expectations, but value you *because* of them. Neither employees nor guests are left guessing about what should be expected (or how far they can push) because focus brings clarity, which brings confidence.

Ritz Carlton is an extreme example, but it's not unusual. Carhartt and Laphroaig are both comfortable advertising their brands' weak spots (fashion and mass appeal, respectively) because they are confident that their audience wants to live on the fringes. Luxury brands like Omega or Tiffany don't shy away from five-figure price tags because they know that's what brings their customer into the store. Costco and Amazon can charge membership fees before you even buy a product because they have the established cachet amongst their audiences to demand it. Even Walmart makes confident decisions, self-assuredly keeping employee pay low and minimizing investment in customer service, because it knows its customer wants the absolute lowest prices. In fact, some would argue that unkempt stores and long lines work to reinforce Walmart's low-price positioning. If you want a pleasant shopping experience, you can go to Target instead.

I once asked a masterful negotiator her secret after watching her work her subject into a far lower price than I would have thought possible. "Simple," she told me. "You have to be willing to walk away." As an industry, funeral service is being out-negotiated. Families are willing to walk away, but you're not. As a result, your brand comes off as desperate and appeasing at the very moment when families most need you to be confident and clear.

The mental space is everything. If a funeral home is unwilling to walk away (or to let a family walk away), then that colors everything else. Its tone will be conciliatory, its bargaining power will be frail, and its brand position will never be one of leadership. As Mitford says, its prices go "down, down, down," and so do its credibility and subject matter authority. When the staff and leadership lose confidence, they're willing to do whatever it takes to get the sale, and the cost is greater than they expect.

But if you choose to focus, if you're willing to walk away, then you put yourself in a position of leadership. The questions in your mind are not, "How do I keep this family?" nor, "How much will I have to give up?" but rather, "Is this family a fit?"; "How do I serve them best?"; and, "What do they really need?" In other words, the confidence that comes from focus doesn't just serve your business; it actually helps you do a better job serving families.

Focus breeds confidence, and confidence breeds focus. We'll talk in Chapter 9 about how you can get there, but just imagine for a moment being able to tell a client, "I'm so sorry, Mrs. Smith. It sounds like you're interested in direct cremation, and we believe as a firm that we exist to provide something more than that. I would love the opportunity to explain our process and why we believe it's important, and if you're not interested, I'd be honored to direct you to a local business who specializes in direct cremation. Since they focus on price and specialize in disposition of the body only, they're a much better choice if you've decided that's what's best for your family."

There are two possible outcomes of this conversation: either Mrs. Smith will acquiesce, and you'll have a chance to present the products and offerings you really want to sell, or she will politely thank you and go elsewhere, and you've saved yourself and your employees the frustration (and cost) of trying to fit a square peg into a round hole for miniscule profit. Either way, Mrs. Smith will be pleasantly surprised by the experience. She will likely tell her friends about it. You will get free advertising. Your employees will be grateful for the line in the sand and the clarity regarding their roles. And you will have stuck to your guns in doing the work that you really want to be doing (whatever that may be).

Most importantly, this virtuous cycle feeds itself. As you turn away more of the work you don't want, your reputation will solidify. You will send a clear signal to your employees, who will begin to work with more confidence and clarity, understanding exactly who and what they should and should not focus on. They will do more of the work you want them to be doing, and that experience will yield expertise. You will also send a clear signal to your market, where a few dozen Mrs. Smiths will inform a few hundred people that somebody in town is doing it right and is willing to help families find the right option, even at cost to themselves. For those people, Mrs. Smith will preach fervently that you are the only option.

You must first muster the confidence to focus. But that focus will pay dividends in additional confidence.

Credibility

Confidence goes hand-in-hand with its sister, credibility.

We all know those restaurants that have phone books for menus. Pasta, pizza, burgers, Asian, Mexican, Mediterranean—all served up out of the same kitchen. At some places, it's good. But it's never *great*. There is a ceiling for the quality of the generic. Menus at the very best restaurants tend to get shorter, not longer.

If you follow the truly great chefs, they specialize. James Beard Award-winner Nancy Silverton obsessed for years over just a few varieties of dough, fine-tuning recipes by making minute adjustments, one variable at a time.[15] What would an extra quarter-teaspoon of salt do? How about another thirty seconds in the oven? Another five degrees? Most hobbyist bakers have made a decent loaf of sourdough. Silverton has invested decades making the perfect sourdough.

Another James Beard winner, Aaron Franklin, chose barbecue—specifically Texas-style barbecue brisket—as his area of focus. Franklin often remarks that the only way to make good barbecue is to make a lot of bad barbecue.[16] And that takes a lot of time and money, which means not spending that time and money on other pursuits. You have to choose what you're good at. Nobody is great at everything, and we lose credibility when we claim to be.

My business partner, Steve McKee, calls this the Michael Jordan Principle.[17] Jordan, arguably one of the greatest athletes of all time, famously failed in his 1994 experimental season with the Chicago White Sox. It's tough to argue that your average MLB player who bested Jordan's eleven errors or .202 batting average had more raw athletic ability. But, McKee explains, "During all those years when Michael Jordan was focusing on basketball, his competitors on the diamond were focusing on baseball."[18] Even the very best cannot master everything. Excellence demands focus.

That is why it strains credibility when a single funeral home says it serves every family who crosses its threshold with excellence. We're talking about one of the most intimate expressions of love and service in the human experience. To do that excellently for one family is a feat. If it's impossible for a single restaurant to excel at both French and Italian cuisine, how much more is it impossible for a company to excel at handling a $30,000 funeral for a devout Baptist community leader and an $800 direct cremation for a transient agnostic widow? You cannot be excellent at both, and nobody believes you when you claim that you are. Nuances will be missed. Details will remain unknown. There will be questions you don't know to ask. A few firms might be able to serve a broad base acceptably. None will ever be able to do so with genuine excellence.

Credibility requires sacrifice. During the thousands of hours Aaron Franklin has spent studying beef and smoke, he has been choosing *not* to study sourdough cultures and dough composition. Nancy Silverton might know a thing or two about barbecue, but her choice to master bread was one and the same with her choice not to invest her time and energy in the finer points of beef brisket. When funeral homes say they're all things to all people, their audiences subconsciously understand that they're mediocre at everything.

This is why the lie of "all things to all people" is so undermining to the funeral home. The very phrase that the calling touts as a badge of honor is perceived by its audience as a strike against it. The time someone says goodbye to their mother is a moment when only perfection will suffice. To detract from a fine dining experience can infuriate a customer; to detract from a grief process is intolerable. This is the moment for the specialists.

You already know this. In some spaces, the death care business has specialization down to a science. We have Catholic cemeteries and Jewish cemeteries catering to specific burial traditions. We have Black, Hispanic, and Asian brands equipped to perform particular rites and make arrangements in particular languages. We have low-cost direct cremation brands and high-end white glove brands, all carefully built and positioned for the right demographics in the right part of town.

But it's what happens in practice, not in theory, that's important. You would probably love to do a direct cremation in your flagship brand, because you know you can charge more on that GPL than if you referred it to your cremation society. And if a family comes into the low-cost storefront but wants to pile on some extras, you're going to celebrate a big win rather than refer them up the chain.

The result, though, is even more confusion and foundational decay than you'd have with one brand. Juggling many brands, each trying to be all things to all people, is even worse than a single brand committed to that lie. Death care brands needlessly sacrifice credibility when they force every specialized storefront to be everything.

The credibility hit is internal first; dissatisfaction grows among employees who are confused regarding their conflicting missions. An employee performing a set of functions under one logo knows he's charging less than the same employee performing the same functions under a different logo. Resentment and confusion fester as people do as they're told, rather than operating with missional clarity and conviction. At worst, the promise of a meaningful career with the purpose of serving families is undermined by the realization that the only real objective is closing the sale.

Families grow confused as well. The luster of selflessness and service can't withstand inconsistent price lists and salesy negotiations. Your beautiful facility and caring words might say that you want to take care of the family, but your business model, your lack of focus, and your deal-making all scream that you just want their cash. The best funeral directors can mollify families and navigate that confusion; the average ones will flounder and exacerbate the problem.

There is a right way to do death. And families are lost, unsure of what that looks like. No one is better equipped to lead and serve them through this moment than you are. But leaders can't be generalists; when they try to be, they sacrifice clarity and credibility. Leaders are focused, sharp, and devoted to their cause. Leading one army means I do so at the exclusion of all others. Leading my family means I place their needs above those of other families. And leading your customers requires that you decide what type of customers you want to lead.

Paradoxically, the challenges driving funeral homes to be generalists (margin pressure, commoditization, complexity) are all better solved by specialization. A focused, confident brand that has decided to be specific things to specific people will be better at serving those people, and better equipped to lead them in their moment of need. And as a result, it will be easier for families to recognize the value you provide, and to appreciate it. It just so happens that the best thing for the families you serve is also the best thing for your business.

Chapter 7

Lie #3: Merchandise Matters.

"A funeral is not an occasion for a display of cheapness. It is, in fact, an opportunity for the display of a status symbol which, by bolstering family pride, does much to assuage grief. A funeral is also an occasion when feelings of guilt and remorse are satisfied to a large extent by the purchase of a fine funeral. It seems highly probable that the most satisfactory funeral service for the average family is one in which the cost has necessitated some degree of sacrifice. This permits the survivors to atone for any real or fancied neglect of the deceased prior to his death."[1]

—*The National Funeral Service Journal*, 1961

Every so often the local or national news will do an exposé on the executive salaries at nonprofit organizations. *Forbes* asked, "Should Non-Profit U.S. Bank Executives Earn Nearly $1 Million Per Year?"[2] *The New York Times* blasted nonprofit hospitals whose CEOs were paid millions during coronavirus furloughs.[3] The *CBS Evening News* reported that one nonprofit executive was on the hook for $20 million in back taxes.[4] In some states, there has even been a push to ban nonprofits from compensating their trustees, after public backlash over what was seen as excessive compensation.[5]

People don't like the idea of mixing service and profit. It's disorienting. It's not that these executives don't earn their paychecks—they may well be just as qualified and work just as hard as their peers at for-profit corporations. But if you tell me that you're motivated by service, and then the curtain is pulled back and the benefits loom larger than the benevolence, I smell a bait-and-switch. Something feels dishonest.

Because of this, funeral professionals are subjected to perhaps the toughest tightrope walk of any business in existence. There's no escaping it, and it's through no fault of your own. To be a mortician is not to be dishonest, and I don't know of any for-profit funeral homes masquerading as a 501(c)3. But nonetheless, the challenge is there. This business comes preloaded with a paradox.

It's what I call "the gap." In its simplest form, it can be summarized as this: the worst day of your customer's life is what feeds your family.

The gap is between the experience, position, and incentives of the bereaved, and the experience, position, and incentives of your firm. And the gap yawns wide the moment the family walks through your door. You didn't want his cousin to die in a car accident, but if she hadn't, you might not have a job. You feel sorry for their loss, but it might be the reason your staff gets a Christmas bonus. You didn't kill her dad, but when she goes home after her funeral, you might congratulate your employee on a job well done. There is a permanent, un-closable gap between the family's perception of death and yours.

Death care professionals did not create this paradox, and it is wrong to fault them for it. Those who look on the calling with suspicion lack the context of the hardship, sacrifice, and service this profession demands. But even though the gap is not your fault, it remains very much your problem.

On the one hand, funeral care is unequivocally a service. Only the most cynical would choose to spend a career with the bereaved and the deceased for no reason but profit. To care for the mortal remains of someone's brother, wife, or friend is a sacred duty—and a difficult one. To comfort the mourning, day in and day out, is truly a calling. I would bet that every one of the people you know who has "washed out" of the profession did so because in some regard they just couldn't handle it. They didn't have the heart, or the stomach. Funeral service is something that absolutely must be done for motivation that runs deeper than a paycheck.

But the paycheck is still there. You are still a business—and you must be. You have overhead, mortgages, employees, taxes, and expenses to worry about. You don't have the protection of nonprofit status or the comfort of an unchallenged market. You have competitors and critics. And you have regulations and regulatory costs. None of this is anything to be ashamed of. Business is a good and effective way to deliver a necessary service. To be profitable at the end of a year means that you have managed your company well and provided value to your community. You should feel nothing for that but a sense of accomplishment and gratitude.

But the gap remains. A funeral home is, unapologetically and of necessity, a business. And yet it is also, humbly and selflessly, a service. Every expectation of society screams that these two cannot—must not—coexist. Yet here we are.

Most in the profession recognize the tension. It's the reason for sincere (if inaccurate) statements like, "We're not an industry; we're a calling." It might be the reason why a gifted and empathetic funeral director just isn't a very good salesman, or why an employee who is outstanding at the management aspects of the business is lousy with families. It's a gap that we will never be able to close—a fissure that will always be there. It might be a source of shame, or of defensiveness, or of apology. But it prevails.

You're not alone. There are other professions whose success relies upon their customers' bad days. Consumers usually only hire a lawyer or a mechanic or a doctor if something is wrong. And those are the bills that we resent the most—they're expensive, unexpected, inconvenient, and non-negotiable. I can't save up for two months before my moment of need. I can't even shop around, really. They've got me cornered and they know it.

The family in your office right now feels just like that, only with the added emotion and pain of a loss, and with the added confusion that comes from visiting a mortuary less frequently than they visit even their mechanic or doctor. We're good at (and comfortable with) the things we do often. But we hardly do this at all.

Again, you didn't make them feel that way. Mitford and her disciples want to blame "the funeral men" for inventing the gap, as though death was originally somehow insulated from economics. But this is ridiculous fiction. People need the work you provide, and you deserve to be paid for providing it. The problem doesn't exist because funeral directors are greedy, exploitative capitalists. It exists because we live in an imperfect world, and funeral directors happen to deal in two realms—death and money—that tend to bring out its deficiencies more than most things in life.

But just as you didn't create it, you can't eliminate it, either. I can't imagine any utopian future for funeral service where having to pay for my loved one's death care is easy or natural. The gap is there, and it will always be there. You can't ignore it, or refine it, or apologize it out of existence. It's a birthmark of the industry, a permanent fixture of the mortician's reality.

What you have to do is respect it. And at times, throughout the history of the calling, funeral professionals have forgotten to do so.

The quotation at the beginning of this chapter was a low point for the calling. For all the flaws in Mitford's argument, here she caught the business red-handed. To claim that overspending on a funeral is therapeutic, or that reconciliation with the deceased can somehow occur by upgrading a casket, is exploitation. It's wrong, and it's the kind of argument that has earned the industry its otherwise undeserved reputation.

There's nothing wrong with an expensive casket if that's what the family really wants, but it's not going to fix their relationship with their father. You might not have ever promised a family that it will, but unfortunately that's not enough, because the industry has a history of erring on this point. The problem that you didn't create was worsened by the greed of your forebears. Silence, therefore, indicates consent—not neutrality.

Relationships with the deceased can't be healed by spending money on a funeral, and it's not good enough for funeral directors to avoid saying they can be. You need to be actively counseling against such thinking. And you need to make that loud and clear, so that it's unmistakable to the public.

Here's why: if you don't, they're going to assume the opposite. They're going to throw you in with the previous generations who got it wrong, and who let self-interest overshadow their calling. They're going to make bad assumptions about you because of the gap, and because of their defensiveness, and because of confusion. As in so many businesses, the sins of the father carry through to subsequent generations, and though the sentiments above about "the purchase of a fine funeral" are thankfully not promoted by the vast majority of mortuaries today, they are still an ugly part of their heritage, and one of which the public is well aware. If you don't renounce and combat this idea, it may yet have strength enough to injure you.

But the most important reason that funeral homes need to speak up about the proper function and role of money in mourning has nothing to do with your own reputation. It has to do with what the family really needs. Consider this: today, you know that the industry was wrong in 1961 when it said that a funeral as a status symbol will assuage grief. But the family may not know. They haven't thought about grief at all— they haven't had occasion to. They've been taught to avoid it. They've been served contradictory and disorienting perspectives from HBO and Hollywood about what funerals are really like. They certainly haven't reflected on which aspects of death care they think are most psychologically valuable. They don't know whether or not an expensive funeral will assuage their grief. *They have no idea what will assuage their grief.*

But they *are* grieving. They don't know what to do, but they are feeling pain. They're unprepared for and unfamiliar with this kind of pain. And they want it gone. When a family sits in your office today, they are less prepared for the experience than any humans in history. On top of the usual numbing and disorienting aspects of grief, they're confused. Frightened. Remorseful. They might be wishing they'd had a different conversation with Dad before he died, or that they had come to visit him sooner. They're wondering what the "right thing" is to do right now. The right thing to atone for past sins. The right thing to honor their loved one. The right thing to help them get rid of this pain. The right thing to get them back to feeling normal again.

All of this places them in an extremely vulnerable position. To some degree, they know this, which is (I believe) the primary reason funeral directors will always be viewed with a level of distrust. There is an element of extreme sensitivity in grief—in its most acute forms, it makes you feel like you've had your skin torn off. And that makes you feel exposed. People instinctively sense they're at risk of being taken advantage of, whether that's the intent of the funeral director or not. So there's an inherent defensiveness at play.

This brings us to merchandise sales. As the service-oriented business of twentieth century funeral homes has waned in demand, merchandise has offered an appealing opportunity for funeral homes to prop up lost revenue. But like the misplaced confidence of "we'll always have the body," or the brand confusion that results from "all things to all people," there are realities and consequences of merchandise sales that the industry generally has been unwilling to acknowledge. And understandably so. Merchandise makes money, so it's easier not to think about its downside. But there is a downside. Merchandise sales aren't inherently wrong, but like other aspects of the business today, it is important to confront the brutal facts of their consequences.

Amidst all of the vulnerability, confusion, lost-ness, and pain that families experience during the funeral planning process, merchandise presents a unique danger, for several reasons. For one, it's secondary. Most families are not meeting with you for the primary purpose of buying products; they're here for services. Funeral homes are primarily in the services business. They exist chiefly to do something *for* you, rather than to sell something *to* you.

What this means is that families understand the services they're buying from you better than they do the products. Nobody has to explain why you need to cremate or bury a body—the need to get that taken care of is what brings the family in the door. The specific value of a viewing or a funeral might bear a little discussion, but usually the balance of information is fairly even here, as well. Families will already know if they want a funeral, and they will already know if considering a viewing is on the table.

Services are also where you have the greatest opportunity to *serve* (the word is no accident). By guiding a lost and confused family through your service offerings, you're helping them understand what must be done, and you're offering a means by which to help them do it. Death brings with it a to-do list, not a shopping list—there are things which necessarily must be done, but not necessarily things which must be bought. Services are closest to the heart of your business because they are closest to the heart of the family's need. This is where you address the most immediate felt needs of your customer and provide the most important guidance and value.

But since merchandise tends to be a secondary need for the family, it's where the balance of knowledge shifts. And so does the balance of value. The family knows why they need to bury Dad; they're much less likely to know why (or whether) he needs a vault. They certainly don't know how to select a vault. They're wholly uneducated on the merits of hardwood versus stainless caskets, let alone 16-gauge versus 18-gauge.

And that's the transition. Once he starts selling products, the funeral director starts *introducing new challenges*, whereas just ten minutes ago, while the discussion was still focused on services, he was helping to eliminate the challenges that the family brought with them.

This matters, because that's the moment the perception of the funeral director changes from ally to obstacle.

All of this, lest we forget, is pressed through the filter of the fact that the customer is grieving a loved one while they're making these decisions. The "fine funeral" quotation is correct in one regard: the survivors are likely processing some "real or fanciful neglect of the deceased," and they are likely looking for some way to "atone."[6] No serious funeral director can argue that a family is objective and rational in this moment. Even the slightest regret, amplified through the megaphone of grief, can lead the family to feel pressure to provide "the best" for their loved one.

A viewing is a decision less about the deceased than the bereaved. Do they need to see Mom, or would they rather avoid that? But the casket feels much more like a gift they're providing *for* her. The funeral director doesn't need to say this or even imply it; the family will get there all on their own. But the funeral director is in a bad spot when he's in the position of either sacrificing revenue (and his averages for the month) or reassuring a family that dropping an extra $3,000 on a casket won't really do anything for their relationship with Mom—nor for their grief process. His incentives are at odds with theirs, and everybody in the room knows it. That tension is something that families will remember when they think about their experience with your funeral home.

Another reason product sales make a bad situation worse is that products are simply of less value to the grief process. If you own a funeral home, you might be predisposed (and financially incentivized) to disagree, but consider objectively which aspects of a funeral you really believe to be most valuable to the family. That's not to say that the others are not valuable at all, nor that you shouldn't sell them. But products are *secondary*, and they should be treated as such.

Through personal experience and compelling accounts from numerous funeral directors, I could readily make a case for the value of a ceremony, or of a viewing, or of memorialization. I've heard hundreds of anecdotes over my life (as, I'm sure, have you) that have convinced me that families benefit greatly from each of these—and from a funeral director's guidance and organization of these processes. But I have yet to hear any evidence that the purchase of a more expensive casket, vault, piece of jewelry, or a thumbprint pocketknife has helped a family to more effectively mourn their loved one to the same extent. You might disagree, but I make this argument entirely out of my esteem for the profession; the services you provide are so valuable that the bar is set high indeed against anyone who wants to argue that products come anywhere close.

Finally, and perhaps most importantly, it's when you're talking about merchandise that you are most vulnerable to being misperceived as a salesman. Merchandise sales are therefore the most important place where you need to "mind the gap." The opportunities for misunderstanding and miscommunication are extreme at the point when people perceive you shifting from confidant to salesperson—when they begin to see you as the millionaire nonprofit executive. That makes it a dangerous moment.

In one focus group I organized, a young man did a sarcastic impression of a funeral director, snapping his fingers and setting his jaw while he sneered, "What can I say to get you into this box?"[7] It's not a coincidence that the casket was the object he dialed in on. When you're sitting in an office or arrangement space, the conversation is focused on the loved one and the services you can provide to honor her. This is an unusual experience, but is often carefully crafted to be comfortable and familial, like a conversation across a dinner table. When you step into the casket selection room, the family immediately recognizes the setting. It's a showroom, a sales space, just like where they go to buy a car or a mattress.

Very few people enjoy the experience of sales showrooms on their sunniest of days. Carvana and CarMax have thrived by offering alternatives to traditional auto dealerships—and to traditional auto dealers. The mattress industry has been disrupted by an explosion of online mattress companies—Nectar, Tuft & Needle, Casper, Saatva, Leesa, Brooklyn Bedding, Purple, Helix,[8] and at least 165 more.[9] Online mattress retail is now a $2 billion dollar industry—an odd concept until you reflect that online options provide an escape from the mattress showroom (and salesman).[10]

As a consumer, the experience of reviewing various models and prices, especially for an expensive product I'll buy only a few times in my life, is awful. The salesman has all of the information, and I have none. I feel like I should know more than I do. I might want to do a little research, but I feel pressure to make a decision on the spot. I might be shocked at the high prices, but I don't want to suffer embarrassment or expose my lack of knowledge.

Again, none of this is your fault; you didn't invent the sales model, and you've likely made efforts to make it less intrusive. But funeral homes shouldn't confuse their lack of culpability with a lack of responsibility. You didn't create all the terrible past sales experiences the family brings with them, but you can't pretend they don't exist, either. Mortuary owners often remind me that their funeral directors aren't paid on commission, as though this is a breakthrough that transforms the experience. It's not. The incentives to sell (and upsell) still exist, and families know it. The value of the product is still murky. The format still mirrors people's most unpleasant purchase experiences. And it's all still amplified by the gap.

Given all of those pressures and pain points, and all of the bad press funeral homes have suffered over the years, I'm surprised that commission ever comes up at all. It's like my doctor reassuring me that he's not paid on commission for the surgery he's telling me I need. I should hope he isn't, and it would be rather appalling if he was. The industry cannot afford to congratulate itself for achieving a modicum of decency.

I often hear two reasons (or defenses) for the importance of merchandise sales. The first is, "They like it." Merchandise sells. People buy what you're peddling. So, the industry reassures itself that it is meeting a demand by providing a product people are looking for. The second is, "We need it." It's harder to make money as a funeral home in the era of direct cremation and the "Nones" than it was in the era of presumed Christian burial, so funeral homes need something to shore up the revenue shortfall.

Both arguments sound compelling on the surface. But neither one stands up to scrutiny.

They like it

One of the tough things about death care is that it is a business without a feedback loop. Amazon sells more than twelve million products; in that setting it's easy to get data on what customers like because they either keep buying or they don't. But when you're selling a once-in-a-lifetime product, there's no way to draw those conclusions. You know what is selling, but not really why. Customers might be buying it because they like it, or because they felt pressured into it, or because they felt guilty for missing last Christmas with Mom. In death care merchandise, the sales case is so isolated that there's no way to extrapolate any meaningful conclusions beyond "they bought it."

Be wary of the assumption that your customers never have buyer's remorse. And, especially when it comes to product sales, don't assume that sales figures indicate product satisfaction. In fact, there's plenty of evidence to suggest that customers don't like being sold to—and that they don't value the products they're being sold as much as you might think.

My firm conducted a major national study that found that people are 50 percent more likely than not to describe funeral homes as rip-offs. Eighty-seven percent of all respondents felt that caskets were overpriced (versus less than 2 percent who said they weren't).[11] It's tough to think of a popular product that only two percent of the population thinks is not overpriced. These responses stood out as by far the greatest complaints about the industry. Merchandise is a much-maligned lightning rod within funeral care as a whole.

Forbes has reported that funeral homes follow "deceptive practices" in their sales approach, a header under which the publication called the industry to task for 289 percent average markups on caskets.[12] An annual survey published by the National Funeral Directors Association found that only a minority of consumers prefer to utilize a full-service funeral home if given the opportunity.[13] A majority said they felt confident that they could plan a funeral without the help of a funeral director.[14] That avoidance isn't a good sign.

In his book *Rest in Peace: a Cultural History of Death and Funeral Homes in Twentieth-Century America*, Gary Laderman documents decades of "hostile"[15] public perceptions of funeral directors as "selfish,"[16] and exploitative, "unscrupulous, mercenary capitalists."[17] He concludes, "In the battle over their public image... funeral directors were simply no match for Jessica Mitford."[18] An independent study conducted on behalf of the Funeral Services Foundation painted a similarly dim picture. Consumers think of funeral directors as controlling, describing them as "tough," "robotic," "rulers," and "bullies."[19] Respondents reported feeling "guilted into costly decisions" by funeral homes who "look like they didn't care about the family."[20]

It's important to pay attention to the specific adjectives used. It's not just that people don't like funeral directors; it's that they perceive them as greedy salesmen—a stereotype overwhelmingly reinforced by the merchandise sales process. People might buy the merchandise, but they clearly do not like the way it's being sold to them. As with nonprofit CEOs, the problem starts when the focus shifts from providing to profiteering.

We need it

More often than, "They like it," I hear the argument that "we need" merchandise sales. Even if customers aren't wild about walking into a casket selection room, the revenue that comes from that part of the process is the only thing keeping the business open. It's a necessary evil.

But this is backwards. Businesses must be built for the customer, not the other way around. Anything else is short-term thinking. When my company consults with any client, one of the first things we do is define the target audience—their needs, wants, likes, and dislikes. Defining who the company is (including what they sell, how they sell it, and how it's priced) doesn't happen until later. If you reverse that order, you're building a business for yourself, and that never works.

Remember Blockbuster and its "managed dissatisfaction?" How about cab drivers, for whom cutting corners and uncomfortable rides were the only ways to stay in business in a cutthroat industry? Kodak could easily have made the case that its decision to bury digital was a necessary evil to protect its film business. The numbers supported all of these decisions—until they didn't. One of the classic blunders in business is to take your eye off the ball. When you're a fresh young industry, everything is built for the customer. But that customer will leave you the moment you turn your gaze inward.

That's why the argument that "we need the money from merchandise" is specious. Merchandise doesn't only cost families money; it costs you trust. It's a temporary gambit to recoup income at a not-insignificant debit to your credibility. Today, merchandise sales are both propping up the roof and eroding the foundation. Funeral home owners should consider carefully whether a short-term revenue boost is worth sacrificing long-term standing.

In the pilot episode of *The Newsroom*, Jeff Daniels' character describes a controversial government program as "a loser" because the cost in reputation outweighs the benefit. "Yeah," he explains, "it accounts for a penny out of our paychecks, but [the other party] gets to hit you with it anytime he wants. It doesn't cost money, it costs votes. It costs airtime and column inches."[21]

The modern funeral home should consider that caskets and especially other merchandise account for a percentage of their paychecks, but also that they cost "airtime and column inches." They cost credibility and trust. They cost your reputation as a servant and as a leader. And Mitford's adherents, from the ones sitting in your chapel right now to the ones at *Time Magazine*, get to hit you with it anytime they want.

There is not a lot of public data available regarding something as specific as merchandise sales per firm, but for the firms whose numbers I've been able to review, figures range from 30-50 percent of total revenue. That is to say, as much as half of the money coming into a funeral home is attached to merchandise sales. It's probably fair to think that's where the argument comes from; not too many businesses could absorb a loss of half their revenue. Not too many would even entertain the idea of tinkering with it. The risk just feels too big.

But that's only part of the story. It's an assumption that this revenue would disappear without merchandise, or with an adjusted merchandise model. It might, but it might come back elsewhere. In fact, if we know that people are spending money that they might not otherwise in a sales process with which they're uncomfortable, imagine what they might spend in a context that made them feel safe and protected.

Accenture published a fascinating and wide-reaching study that quantified the revenue impact of trust. By studying more than 7,000 companies in more than twenty industries, Accenture found that a decline in trust is quantifiably tied to spending—to the tune of hundreds of billions of dollars.[22] In one case, a B2C company with a single publicity event gone wrong suffered a correlated $400 million drop in revenue and a $200 million EBITDA loss.[23] In one industry, trust was linked to fluctuations of more than 20 percent of a company's revenue.[24]

A move that seeks to restore that trust—even by sacrificing one of the revenue streams that is hurting it—could be profitable in itself. In fact, you can win a lot of credibility with a client by showing that you're willingly accepting pain to alleviate theirs.

Southwest Airlines' "Bags Fly Free" campaign represents one of the greatest insights in the history of marketing. Nobody likes buying a plane ticket when they know that the ticket price isn't really the ticket price—you'll pay at least another $50 at the gate in what feels like robbery. The mainstream airlines have all concluded that they have to do it—their industry is feeling the squeeze from every direction, and bag fees represent a chunk of revenue with which they'd rather not part. But Southwest tells its customer (to paraphrase), "We know those fees are awful, so we'll take a $50 hit every time you fly, just to save you from the pain." Every time I fly Southwest, I can't help but feel sorry for those suckers in all of the other lines pulling out credit cards to check their bags. That's the power of empathy in branding.

The eTrade Baby, another marketing classic, often poked fun at "big expensive brokers."[25] That was the genius of eTrade: it recognized that the existing model, with opaque fees and cumbersome structures, was painful for customers. So, eTrade used early digital technology to cut through the pain and offer customers an alternative. Even the cute and entertaining (not to mention hilarious) "spokesbaby" cut against the grain of the industry and invited frustrated customers into a better experience.

Both approaches should have been costly. Southwest willingly sacrifices its slice of a $5 billion baggage-fee pie every year.[26] And eTrade abandoned all of the traditional wisdom of how to make money in trading. But Southwest has been called by investors "the most likely to survive" whenever the airline industry has faced stiff headwinds,[27] and eTrade helped redefine online investing, ultimately leading toward a trend of zero commissions industrywide.[28]

None of this is to say that you have to give up merchandise altogether. But there might be opportunities to rebuild trust by recognizing those revenue streams that are damaging it—and reconsidering or adjusting them accordingly.

On the one hand, funeral homes are in a somewhat favorable position to make changes to their model because they have so many different revenue streams available. You can tinker with casket sales, or with third-party merchandise, or with service offerings, each without impacting the other aspects of your business (or perhaps with favorable results in other parallel streams). Many comparably sized businesses don't have this luxury; a grocery store sells groceries, and a change to how it does so is an all-or-nothing gamble.

But this advantage is only an advantage if you use it. If you're not looking for opportunities to take risks and improve, and if you consider every revenue stream to be fixed and non-negotiable, then your diversification will atrophy into a liability. If you're not acting like an entrepreneur, testing and prototyping, then your multiple revenue streams simply represent multiple line items on a receipt—and multiple opportunities for a family to conclude that they got taken for a ride.

Families don't really know what to make of a funeral home. You're part event planner, part grief counselor, part agent, and part merchandise dealer. It's tough to be good at all of those things, and it's tough for the family to understand (let alone value) your role as you ping-pong between them. In that sense merchandise is a distraction, taking your eye off the ball and robbing you of your ability to serve the family as well as you could if you were focused on service alone.

Or, to couch the question in even higher terms: what does merchandise sales do for the right way to grieve? Does your role as casket salesman make you better or worse equipped to lead a bewildered family toward good mourning? If you were to build from scratch a new business to help confused and uninitiated people do death right, would it include a prominent casket selection room? If a family is in denial over a loss and you're trying to help them confront its reality, is the Legacy Touch display in your office a boon to that process or an interruption?

And, if there really is a right way to grieve, are there opportunities for profits more closely aligned to that aim that could offset the merchandise revenue you've come to depend upon? If you're focused on product sales at the very moment families are most desperately in need of guidance and expertise, you might be getting it backward. The modern funeral home sells products that families value little, while giving away services ("first call" orientation and guidance, aftercare, preplanning consultation, and others) that represent the greatest value and the highest demand among customers.

Mixed priorities are a problem. If I tell you I need your donations to help starving children, and then you find out I live in a thirty-million-dollar house, something is amiss. If you train your funeral directors to help families grieve in a healthy way but also to sell the most product, sooner or later they're going to have to make a choice between those two priorities. There are conflicting interests at play, and families will recognize it.

Because of the gap, because of society's disorientation when it comes to how to do death right, and because of the industry's less-than-perfect past in merchandise sales, funeral service has no room for error. In any business, misaligned incentives are a problem. In this business, they're fatal. If product sales are ancillary to your business, that's fine, and even beneficial. But it will take a lot of intentionality to keep them there—to not confuse them with the core mission, nor to let them detract from it.

Families don't like being sold to. They don't need more stuff. And you don't need the revenue. You might think you do, but that's one of the lies of addiction. Funeral homes are hooked on the narcotic of product sales, and withdrawals might be nasty—even fatal for some firms. But the long-term effects of the addiction are even worse.

Like a drug, excessive merchandise sales may be costing your firm its health, its credibility, and its trustworthiness. But you can get clean. If and as you move beyond overdependency on a broken and polluted revenue stream, you will be able to focus—really focus—on serving families again. You will be able to earn families' trust again. You will be able to get healthy as a business again. And you will be able to make something happen that is more important and more rewarding than all of these things. Families will once again look to you for leadership and guidance in their grief. And you will be able to help them heal again.

Section 3: The Solution

Chapter 8
How We Work

A business model might be summed up as the intersection of three components: how we work, how we make money, and how we sell. If each of these variables is clearly defined, the business itself begins to take shape.

What follows in the next three chapters is not intended to be *the* solution for death care. Real change in the business can only happen through implementation—theory alone is not enough. And any solution will need to be custom-built for the given markets and strengths of your specific business; what works for Glenn Funeral Home in Kentucky might look very different from what works for Miller-Jones in California. What I do hope to provide is a compass—principles that can be used to help think through and address the challenges presented in the previous section.

In many respects, the idea that "we'll always have the body" is a statement about the first prong of a business model: how we work. Funeral homes—and indeed, the death care business as a whole—have historically been defined around the body. Training in mortuary school focuses heavily on embalming and preparation of the deceased. As already discussed, most of the industry's revenue sources are tied to the body. A mortuary's work begins and ends with the body; first calls deal primarily with bringing the body into the care of the funeral home, and little work remains to be done after a burial, scattering, or transfer of the remains back into the care of the family.

Imagine sitting down and creating a new business model for your funeral home today. If you wanted it to look like it does today, you might write "the body" under the heading of "How we work." You're working within a model where "possession is nine-tenths." You start working when you pick the body up and stop working when you no longer have it. You'll sell products to hold the body, preserve the body, display the body, and remember the body. You'll even sell the body back to me *as* a product, should I wish to capture its fingerprints, place it in a sapling's roots, or turn it into jewelry.

The great irony of all this is that any funeral director will tell you that the funeral is *not* for the deceased. That's true, and funeral professionals should remember it. And here we see one of the great cracks in the entire business model: it has been built around the wrong target audience. The deceased doesn't benefit from your offerings. Nor does he choose them (most of the time). Nor does he pay for them. And yet, if you were to write a new GPL with the rule that every product or service must be primarily oriented around the *bereaved* rather than the *deceased*, I would bet that it would not be the GPL you have today.

All of this comes into focus as the body falls out of vogue. Memorial services where the body is not present are staggeringly popular today. Two-thirds of Americans are interested in cremation, and of those, only a quarter say they would want a funeral with the body present prior to cremation.[1] Remarkably, among the remainder, the majority would choose to either have a service with a photograph instead of the urn, or to have no service at all. Even having an urn with cremated remains present is the preference of only a minority, indicating (astonishingly) that the body, even a cremated body, is of rapidly diminishing importance to the modern death care customer.

That rapidity can hardly be overstated. In 2010, half of adults over the age of 40 owned cemetery property.[2] Today, not only do your customers not own cemetery property, they don't even want a memorial service with cremated remains present. Change is happening fast, and more change is coming. It's not enough to simply update or reinvent today. A successful business must be built for *constant* reinvention, so that specifics like the body never become entrenched distractions.

To survive, mortuaries will have to keep up with whiplash-inducing changes in the industry. There's nothing inherently wrong with a mortuary providing products and services to deal with a dead body; this has a reasonable and commonsense connection to your work. But an excessive focus on the body itself has prevented the industry from adopting three vital components in its business model: urgency, agility, and consumer-centrism.

Urgency is important because it's an ingredient of any startup—and it's the ingredient that businesses near their demise tend to lack. When you're a small, scrappy new entrant to any industry, there are few sacred cows. Older, more established firms steadily become more cumbersome and unable (or unwilling) to pivot when needed. As we've seen, Blockbuster, Kodak, taxi companies, and Blackberry all lacked urgency in addressing core problems because they didn't perceive new challengers as a credible threat. As a result, they were too slow to adapt.

Agility, therefore, can be a useful byproduct of urgency. The industry's historic link to a single aspect of its work—body preparation—has led to hesitancy to move decisively into other areas or opportunities as they become available. The British men's eight crew team famously won gold in Sydney by evaluating every decision through a single question: "Will it make the boat go faster?"[3] You don't worry about questions like that unless you think the competition has a good chance of beating you. But a willingness to put anything on the table in service of a singular mission is what made the team adaptable—any change to strategy, training, diet, team composition, or boat design was worthy of consideration as long as it would make the boat go faster. For funeral homes to win today, they will need to rebuild themselves for similar agility and adaptability.

And all of this must be in the service of the family. "We'll always have the body" is most worrisome because it establishes a posture of protected aloofness rather than one of humble willingness to serve. As the family becomes less desirous of services related to the body, you must be willing to provide the services they do desire. And more importantly, as the family becomes increasingly distanced and bewildered by end-of-life preparations as a whole, body preparation ceases to be the most important service that you can provide. Embalming and care for the deceased were good priorities when society inherently understood the value of those services. As culture has regressed in that knowledge, the guidance and counsel that would have been unnecessary and even insulting a generation ago might today become your greatest value to the family.

Let's look at each of these three components in more detail.

Urgency

Sir George Buckley is the former chairman, president, and chief executive of 3M. Under his leadership, 3M became one of business' more famous turnaround stories, which cemented Buckley's reputation as a commanding authority on business strategy. He famously observed that "the core of every business is dying."[4]

It's a startling revelation from a man whose reputation lies in keeping businesses alive. You might have expected him to identify the core of 3M, and then explain how that core was the key to its survival. But, it turns out, Buckley was able to save companies by recognizing their mortality.

Rodney Zemmel, a senior partner at McKinsey, editorializes further on Sir George's observation:

> Every business has a dying core because that's the old heart of the business. The only way you're ever going to be able to grow the business is by making sure you have the balance right between how you manage the decline or the stability of the core and what you do in new areas.[5]

To put it bluntly, the body is already dead. But the core business it represents for your mortuary is dying. And the only way your funeral home will grow is to balance how to manage its decline, not protect its permanence. That's not to say you should stop doing embalming tomorrow. But success will rely on positioning your firm for agility, which means holding your core mission tightly while holding the specifics of its delivery—including the body—loosely.

To "manage the decline of the core" requires a fundamental mindset shift to one of urgency. If your core is immortal, there is little urgency to make changes to your business; that's why the "always" part of "we'll always have the body" is so dangerous. But if you recognize that your business model is always in a state of continuous decay, and that only active, engaged change can prolong its life, your position shifts entirely.

A dear friend of mine who started his own business once remarked, "I used to think that being an entrepreneur meant taking a risk and, if you make it, you make it. What I have come to learn is that being an entrepreneur means taking a risk and, if you make it, all that does is qualify you to take another (often bigger) risk. And another and another."

In other words, despite the substantial successes and longevity of your business, you have not yet arrived. You never will. Like every other business owner, you are responsible for something that is inherently mortal and must be fed and nurtured if it is to be kept alive.

Funeral homes built around the body have simply been outmaneuvered. That doesn't mean they were wrong to focus on the body; such a focus made a lot of sense for a long time. But the moment it's no longer a focal point—when cremation dominates, when memorial services supersede funerals, and when religious and cultural traditions no longer demand it—the business must be willing to shift.

In the prologue to *Antifragile*, author Nassim Taleb describes his concept:

> Some things benefit from shocks; they thrive and grow when exposed to volatility, randomness, disorder, and stressors and love adventure, risk, and uncertainty. Yet, in spite of the ubiquity of the phenomenon, there is no word for the exact opposite of fragile. Let us call it antifragile. Antifragility is beyond resilience or robustness. The resilient resists shocks and stays the same; the antifragile gets better.[6]

Funeral homes are indisputably a fragile business model. The final blow has not yet been dealt—the stressors or changes that could shatter the business have not yet arisen. But it's difficult to argue that funeral homes are resilient to change; they have survived mounting cultural transformations only insofar as those transformations have not yet become universal.

Traditional mortuaries haven't figured out a way to garner significant profits from direct cremation; they're only succeeding because of the families who still don't want direct cremation. They haven't figured out a way to remain relevant to those families who prefer an at-home memorial service; they only continue to profit as long as some number of families prefer a traditional funeral. But should the winds blow harder in those directions, the business is dead. It's already dying.

Still, if antifragility is indeed possible, there would be no better application of it than in funeral service. Your customer is confused, lost, tired, grieving, and emotional. There are few stages in life during which "volatility, randomness, disorder, and stressors" are so certain as during grief. So, if funeral homes can conceive of a model that is *antifragile* in the face of those stressors—that is, a model that is better, stronger, and more useful the more confused, volatile, and disordered the situation becomes—then they will create a far more reliable and beneficial future.

This is where "the right way" becomes important. The relevance of the industry has been tied to the relatively unimportant. Whether or not the industry "has the body" is a petty concern against the backdrop of a family's overall grief. If a business ties its relevance to a specific circumstance (whether burial rates remain high, whether licensing requirements for funeral directors are protected) then it will be relevant only as long as that circumstance is relevant—and it will become irrelevant the moment it is not. On the other hand, if it connects its relevance instead to fundamental truths about human needs (which don't change), then it will be in a much more resilient position.

One of the greatest threats that stems from a lack of urgency is the most tangible. You might not think of succession as a decision about your firm's business model, but the reality is that nothing has such a great impact on your firm's business model—and its ability to improve—as decisions around who is at the helm.

The number of funeral homes without any succession plan in place, or who have obviously delayed succession for decades too long, is astounding. I know owners well into their sixties who have not yet considered their own succession plans, and owners in their eighties who are still struggling to let go. The people who work closest to death, it would seem, are the least cognizant of their own mortality.

As a rule of thumb, your fifties are the perfect time to finalize and implement your succession strategy. By the time you turn sixty, you should be active in the business (should you so choose), but no longer an owner. This is not because of a lack of relevance or knowledge; I wish businesses had far *more* sixty-, seventy-, and eighty-year-olds in place to provide the advice and perspective that younger generations lack. But it's simply an inescapable truth that by the time you're into your sixties, your perspective is different. You might be thinking about the future, but it's no longer *your* future. The urgency and immediacy of important business decisions require skin in the game. They require a leader whose future and personal wealth are directly tied to the health of the business, not only today, but twenty years from now.

Moreover, deferred succession needlessly complicates the decision-making process. The heat of battle demands a single leader and a clear chain of command. Shared decision-making power creates delays, indecision, and deadlocks that are fatal to business. Again, to have a former generation (or two) on hand as trusted advisors is an invaluable gift to the business. But to grant those advisors veto power turns their blessing into a liability.

It's worth noting that the same principle applies outside of succession. It's acceptable—beneficial, even—for a firm to have multiple owners. But if there is no majority owner, or at the very least one individual with clearly defined decision-making power over the rest, your firm is likely sacrificing speed and agility at the moment it can afford neither. You don't want the moment of crisis to be the time you find out that your owners are not aligned on the future of the business. And you certainly don't want that moment to be the one when you're stymied by gridlock.

It's never too early to begin planning your succession. Would a sale to a big conglomerate be a failure? Or a success? (There's no right answer here; every owner must answer that question for themselves.) Is there a family member waiting in the wings and ready to take over? Is it time to stop kidding yourself and accept the fact that your son or daughter will never go into the family business? Are you ready to grieve and let go of your family's ownership of this place?

Good succession usually involves at least two steps. An attorney and a CPA can help you navigate the mechanics of succession, but likely not the principles. Before hiring those general contractors to build the house, you first need to design it. And the design will be a process, not a moment. This likely requires a lot of thinking, difficult conversations, introspection, and honesty.

But it's not something to put off. The length and complexity of the succession process is exactly why it must start now. And once it's done, your efforts will pay dividends for the firm through the clarity and agility required to navigate the difficult waters ahead.

Succession is a practical step taken at the micro level—a contract between predecessor and successor. But your firm likely also has work to do at the macro level, in terms of revisiting the contracts between your firm and its governing authorities, particularly at the state level.

Protectionism is the last defense of irrelevant industries. Automakers were once the pride of American business; today they are a source of derision and frustration thanks to the notion of "too big to fail" and everything that means for taxpayers and customers.

The exacting regulations that for decades protected funeral homes from upstart competition today prevent those same funeral homes from pivoting the way they need to. It might be time to consider lobbying *against* those protections at the state level. For one, this could place you in a position of leadership. Unless you're certain that these regulations are here to stay (and you can't be), then dismantling them on your terms is far better than watching them be reconfigured by an enemy with an axe to grind. Moreover, a well-executed PR campaign, in which you seek to sacrifice your protections in the service of consumers, would be an outstanding way to get in front of an inevitable PR campaign from your opponents, who will doubtless seek to paint you as part of a crooked industry in need of even further regulation.

It might be what families need, too. If nobody's benefitting from state-mandated casket selection rooms, embalming regulations, and on-site prep rooms, it's time to argue on their behalf for something different. And if you're successful, it could free up overhead and open new doors to provide new products and services that families really want.

This could be done through your state boards and associations. It will take courage to lead the charge, but the very organizations that historically have stood against change might be those with the position and influence to promote it. Or, you might consider hiring a lobbyist yourself.

A public relations or marketing campaign to repeal outdated regulations may support or even replace lobbying efforts.

Lest this sound radical, consider the likelihood that it will happen, sooner or later. Few industrial protections last forever, and fewer still for unpopular and misunderstood industries. If repeal is going to happen, far better that it happen under your guidance. Had taxis been willing to sacrifice regulatory protection, they would doubtless have been better prepared for Uber. But more importantly, passengers might have liked what they were getting from taxis enough that Uber never would have taken off.

Such is the footing of a business operating with urgency. As long as we assume the gravy train is infinite, we will be hesitant to make changes. But if we recognize that it's going to end, then we will begin to make the moves necessary to thrive when it does.

Agility

One of the simplest ways to foster a resilient culture of adaptation is through *engagement*. Funeral home owners tend to underestimate the impact they have on their staff. The context of the business and the gravitas of the work leads staff to idolize their leadership. I've interviewed countless entry- and mid-level staff who can recall an insight or a piece of instruction about funeral service that their manager or president shared with them a decade ago. And yet, whether out of a desire to not tread too heavily on what their forebears have built, or simply because they're more comfortable one-on-one with families than in addressing large groups, oftentimes I see owners struggle to envision themselves as active leaders within their firms.

There is a military doctrine that has been employed successfully by countries that are inherently in defensive positions, facing imminent threat of invasion by numerous enemies. Because of the high stakes and the speed required to react to changing situations quickly, under the philosophy of "mission-type tactics," orders focus on *intent* rather than *tactics*, and the subordinate is given broad autonomy as to how to execute. For example, an order to take a hill would also include information as to why the hill is important, and by when it must be taken. The subordinate receiving the order then has the independence to decide how to go about taking the hill—and even, should conditions change, *whether* to take it. This ensures that the order is carried out in a manner consistent with its spirit and objective, even if the situation changes.

Funeral service is in a defensive position, facing threat of invasion by numerous enemies. But generally, it operates in a manner opposite from mission-type tactics. Orders are direct and constrained: "sell this product" or "hit this sales goal," with little focus on the broader context of the business need or the utility to the family. In other words, far more emphasis is placed on the *how*—how to embalm a body or how to plan a funeral—than the *why*. As a result, employees have limited space to innovate or pivot, and specific directives often outlast their purpose or need.

On the other hand, mortuary leaders who focus on instilling a philosophy and a heart of service in their employees will equip those teams with the tools to better meet families' needs and invent new solutions as they're needed.

Active, consistent guidance to your staff literally has the power to change lives. Unlike dictatorial order-barking, equipping your team with a philosophy of service, and continuously reiterating (or revising) that philosophy, can work wonders. This might be a monthly email in which you describe trends in the industry along with your thoughts about how your firm will address them. Or all-company meetings in which you highlight examples of particularly successful services and the principles behind why they went so well. If you assume that your business model is permanent and fixed, communicating this way is either unnecessary (because you already told employees) or daunting (because of the pressure of perfection). But if you assume that you lead a constantly changing workforce in a continually changing environment, it would stand to reason that your team would need regular reminders and reassurance about what they do and why they do it.

It is important to focus here on principles rather than procedures. A GPL change or process update are important and need to be communicated. But keeping your team coached on the principles *behind* those mechanisms will help them operate with clarity and autonomy, not waiting for direction but instead helping to build and deliver the company you want. Always be on the lookout for opportunities to engage with and lead your team, so that they can understand and further your objectives under your guidance and with the benefit of your perspective.

Another way to evolve how you work, and to move toward a more agile business model, is to take small risks. According to *Harvard Business Review*, the concept of "*parallel play*, exploring and testing their world the way young children do,"[7] is a key success factor among startups. Obviously it's not reasonable to expect a century-old business with a century-old business model to investigate every aspect of its business as a young child would. However, looking for micro-opportunities to explore and test can be a valuable source of invention.

When my team approached Sunset Memorial Park with the concept for Scatter Day, we were nervous. I wasn't sure they would go for it. After all, we were recommending that a for-profit cemetery promote an event encouraging scattering free of charge. But to the Sunset Memorial team's great credit, they saw it as a relatively small risk. There were promotional costs involved, but it was a single event—we weren't asking them to roll out a new business model overnight. Scatter Day turned out to be a great success, and Sunset's parent company has since applied learnings and principles gleaned from that adaptation to other events and improvements.

It can be tempting to think of business transformation as a singular, monolithic event. But rarely, if ever, has this actually been the path of improvement. Instead, being on the lookout for small risks to take is a paradigm-transforming exercise that puts you on offense and does so in bite-sized pieces. To transform your entire company in one fell swoop is both overwhelming and probably unwise. But getting off defense and actively seeking adaptations, however small, is vital.

Schoedinger Funerals & Cremation Service in Ohio has long been a firm I admire. Its website reads as a list of small risks. Schoedinger was one of the first firms to roll pet services under its primary brand. The site boasts an innovative preplanning tool that allows families to make prearrangements digitally. GPLs are displayed online—a move that is terrifying to many similarly-priced firms. Each of these decisions represented a small risk that strayed slightly from the beaten path. Notably, any could have been abandoned just as easily if they had turned out to be bad moves, and all could be invested in further to the extent they show promise. As the old saying goes, "You never know until you try."

Funeral home owners may be at a disadvantage because the finality of a funeral is so very much at odds with the ongoing nature of business. To run a funeral well means to execute perfectly (flaws mean failure) within a finite period of time. But to run a business well is exactly the opposite; momentum beats perfection, and there is no end date. Decisions can be reconsidered at any time, and mistakes are inevitable but rarely fatal. Successful funeral home owners might do well to encourage, in their management of the company, the very sort of innovation, risk-taking, and acceptance of failure that would be disastrous in the management of a funeral.

How might you tinker with your GPL? What new services do you want to try out? What did a family ask for last month that you weren't able to deliver? What functionality could be added to your website? What idea did an associate share with you last month that might be worth a few thousand dollars to test? Where might you be able to hire an expert to solve a problem for you? Worst case scenario, you invest in a few offerings or approaches that your competitors don't have. Best case, you're the only survivor.

These small risks might be best taken by what you could politely call "imitation." Funeral service is an interesting category, in that it exists internationally but still competes (for the most part) locally. Independent firms, with their national networks and unhindered autonomy, can invent and swap ideas quickly. If a colleague in Minneapolis tries something in the spring, you could implement it in your firm in Dallas by the fall.

Most funeral homes peg their marketing budgets to a revenue figure, such as five percent of the previous year's sales. But what if you had an annual innovation budget? Shift your thinking from *whether* you'll invest in innovation to *how* you will invest in innovating. If you set aside even one percent of last year's total revenue and commit that money to a few experiments, you'll find yourself in a whole new mindset. Stagnancy is the enemy, and momentum requires change. Viewing that change through the lens of small, incremental improvements that can be retracted or extended based on their success is a far more practical and accessible path to evolution than an approach of all-out overnight transformation.

Consumer-centrism

The context of all of these decisions—succession, lobbying, risk-taking, internal engagement—must be the family. Reject the mindset of, "We'll always have the body" in favor of the mindset, "We must always earn the family." This is about getting in the back of the cab and looking around—not through the eyes of a seasoned professional, but through the eyes of the emotional and disoriented families you serve.

No doubt you've done this already. Funeral homes that have torn out pews in their chapels, or added "cremations" to their signage in the early 2000s, did so with an eye to the family and their needs. But it's important that changes aren't merely cosmetic; transformation must go deep.

This is rooted in a trait you already know well: empathy. You empathize with a family's pain related to the death of their loved one every day;

consider how you can empathize with their pain related to your business model. Erase all of your assumptions and understanding of the business as an insider, and put yourself in the position of an outsider. You've just lost a parent. You've possibly never been to a funeral before—likely not in the last decade. You're afraid of being taken advantage of. You don't have tens of thousands of dollars lying around, and you resent the expenses you know are coming. You're stressed and distracted by all of the tasks, guests, and opinions flying around in your mind. You met a funeral director once who you didn't particularly trust, and he became for you the archetype of the profession. You don't mind making arrangements, but you're dreading getting upsold and having to say no over and over again. You're intimidated by your lack of experience and knowledge. You loved your mom, but you don't know what decisions will do right by her. You know you want to honor her with this last opportunity, but you have no idea what that looks like. You know, no matter what, that you can't mess it up.

Now, in that mindset, walk through every step of the process. Start at the website—does the first thing it says make the introduction you want to make? Do they want to read about how your great-grandfather started the business 85 years ago? Are they able to find—easily and quickly—the information they're really looking for? Does it resonate with them emotionally?

Next, your office. Is it designed to put them at ease and remove burdens? Does it create any new burdens, physical or psychological? What steps or processes might seem odd or off-putting to an outsider, even if you understand why they're important?

And, most importantly, consider your leadership. If a family is lost, confused, skeptical, and uneducated, are you guiding them? Do you approach them with a spirit of winsome authority, gently and humbly shepherding them through a process about which you are an expert and they know nothing? Are your offerings made completely in their interest, even to the point that you're willing to make sacrifices to accommodate their needs?

Where might they suspect—even if wrongly—self-interest on your part?

To give a family what they want is one thing. To sell to them is another. But to lead, such that you impart the comfort, confidence, and peace of mind that comes from selflessness, is something else entirely. Consider carefully which results your processes yield.

The way in which a modern funeral home works was historically built around the body. But what if it were built around the family? What if you started working for the family as a consultant, advisor, and guide the moment they first contacted you, rather than doing so only as an end to "bring the loved one into our care?" What might your services look like if your GPL was built primarily around care for each individual member of the family—siblings, children, cousins, and friends—rather than primarily around care for the deceased? Do you have a product and service line that's built for—not that will merely accommodate, but that is *really* built for – a family that actually wants to follow every key step of the grief process, but wants to do so at home rather than in your chapel?

Are you prepared to help a family memorialize if they don't want to do so at a cemetery? Do you have services ready for a family who shares with you that they're struggling to let go a month after a burial? Do you have a product to help a family anticipate and plan for the needs of grief before the moment of need? Do you have a business relationship and rate card with every local pub, park service, and bowling alley so that you can recommend creative solutions the moment you find out that the deceased was a whiskey connoisseur, fly fisherman, or bowler?

Do you have products and services built for the disappointed golf buddy who didn't get to say goodbye to his friend because his wife didn't plan a funeral? Do you have online planning software that will let a family collaborate together from different parts of the world? Can a family enter details in your online database ahead of time so that the in-person meeting is more efficient—and so that your associates can come prepared with tailor-made recommendations?

Most importantly, how would your staff react to requests for each of the above? Would they see these as opportunities to amaze and support a grieving family in need? Or would they be bewildered and frustrated with requests for which they have no category and are unprepared to handle? The answers reveal whether your firm is truly built for the families you serve.

This is the most basic of starter lists. But every one of these innovations (and hundreds more not listed here) are ways you can rethink how you work with the family. In 1920, coming into the funeral parlor for a two-hour meeting made a lot of sense. But in the century since, nearly every business transaction has been transformed—families expect funeral homes to be equally accommodating.

During the COVID-19 outbreak and subsequent quarantines, I made a point of patronizing a local restaurant owned by a friend. One day, as I was stopping by for takeout, I asked how he was doing. "We're actually hanging in there!" he said enthusiastically. He then explained that he had launched contracts with a number of essential businesses to provide in-house catering for their staff, and was pulling out all the stops so that he, his wife, and his brother could make deliveries while his staff handled takeout orders. I was impressed by his hustle, but I'll never forget what he said next. "Yeah, these businesses told me that they called several of our competitors before us, but they said they didn't deliver."

I found out a month later that two of the competitors he named had closed for good. Meanwhile, my friend repurposed part of his kitchen to make gourmet sausage for customers to grill at home over the summer as yet another way to roll with the punches. He continued to thrive, even as the lockdowns dragged on. His recognition of the urgency of the situation, coupled with his ability to find ways to react with agility, made him the most proactive and sensitive to his customer's needs. He didn't stick to his old business model when his customers' situation and expectations changed; he changed with them. And therefore, he was the most successful.

That kind of work requires great empathy. Sympathy is cheap. To look on at another's position and feel sorry for them is something anyone can do. But empathy—to understand and *share* the feelings of another—is no easy feat. This is especially true when their feelings might be of distrust or even hostility toward you.

But empathy is vital to your success in defining your company's business model for the next century. To recognize that your customer is not a sure thing, and that their changing needs must be met by offerings and services that change with them, will require great sacrifice. It will also set you apart from your competitors and enable you to thrive while they falter.

Consider your firm's history. A century ago, there was likely nobody in your hometown with the role of undertaker. Families might have had to handle preparations of the body, dig a grave, contact loved ones, and organize the funeral all on their own. This was challenging and time-consuming, and a distraction from the process of grief. Your founder recognized that and *met a need*. He was likely unconcerned with optimization, case counts, and averages; he just built a business that offered the things families were looking for. Most of them might not have had their own horse and carriage, which is why many early funeral homes invested in a stable. The offerings of the company matched the needs of the customer.

Today, success requires nothing less. In fact, it requires a good deal more, because what a family wants is often not what they truly need. As a result, your products and services must find ways to address both, solving immediate challenges while also setting families up for long-term health. To tackle such a complex project with century-old equipment is unlikely to be effective. So, like your founder, you will need to take a close look at the families you serve and rebuild your business around their needs.

You might not have the tools to do so. You'll probably have to invent some if you want to succeed. But you do have a unique advantage: today, you are the only one with the experience, knowledge, and expertise that invention will require. Better to start now before somebody else figures it out.

Chapter 9
How We Sell

If how you work is vital to the delivery of your firm's products and services, then how you sell is vital to how families understand you—even before they walk in the door. In fact, the word "sell" itself is loaded. As we've already discussed, funeral homes tend to rely on a heavily sales-centric approach, which brings its own assumptions and consequences to the table. Rethinking "how we sell" really requires more than sales alone. It means reconsidering some of the most foundational aspects of your business.

As we discussed in Chapter 6, the attitude that a funeral home must be all things to all people is detrimental to its long-term success as a brand. Sales efforts built on such an approach are destined to falter. Effective brands focus. And if your mission involves shepherding a lost generation back toward healthy grieving, you absolutely must be positioned as a leader—something that is impossible if you give in to desperation and seek to win any and all business that comes your way.

For any company, there are two prongs to a successful go-to-market strategy: sales and marketing. The former includes one-on-one, direct, relational engagement at the moment of consideration—a representative actively engaging with a customer about a potential purchase of a product or service. But marketing is a much broader concept and can have a significant impact before, during, and after the moment of purchase. Marketing includes the "four Ps:" Price, Promotion, Product, and Place. It includes the advertising that brings families in the door, but also decisions as fundamental as what you sell, how much you charge for it, and where you do business. Focusing on sales alone is a costly error because it keeps you from experimenting with and fine-tuning all these other key variables.

For most funeral homes, both marketing and sales are based in a scarcity mindset (all things to all people) and are therefore grounded in a position of disadvantage. Success for both bottom-line business goals and excellent service to families requires that sales and marketing operate from a leadership position, which both presumes and requires a focused target.

On the sales side, this will usually involve some kind of portfolio approach by which the *company* operates broadly within a market while its *brands* are clearly focused on different aspects of the market. This is a strategy that many funeral homes have already adopted nominally, but generally struggle to execute well in practice.

All of this, of course, requires an actual investment in marketing. Funeral homes are notoriously hesitant to devote resources to marketing for their firms. They often cap marketing investment at arbitrary and insufficient levels and invest in unsophisticated channels that produce low return on investment. Both a reason for and a result of this is the exceptional pressure that is placed on sales, the traditionally overworked half of the equation.

A shift of energy and resources from sales to marketing can create a more successful and balanced sales equation, relieve pressure on the sales team, and build a more successful, more credible, less strained brand. But to effectively make this shift requires intentional upstream decisions to position your brand to serve (and sell to) a specific, focused target audience.

It's been said that success in business isn't defined by the business you get, but rather by the business you turn away. Being in the position to decline work from customers who aren't a good match for your offerings signifies a great achievement that only the most confident, well-established brands can afford. Often, this is a self-fulfilling prophecy. The brands with the discipline to turn away work earn the credibility and confidence needed to attract more of their core customers. The brands that desperately take any work that comes their way foster only confusion and self-doubt.

In funeral service, it's an inescapable truth that demand is limited. The industry didn't invent a scarcity mindset; there is an actual reality of scarcity in your business. Thus, a single brand that focuses on a particular target is necessarily sacrificing business to others that attempt to cast a wider net. That's a sobering reality, and not one to ignore.

However, it is possible to adopt a strategy that achieves both focus and breadth. It's complicated and can be expensive to implement well, but it is remarkably effective. And if done properly the return far outweighs the investment.

We've already discussed Procter & Gamble's marketing prowess in Chapter 6. And while the company's massive investment in marketing is noteworthy, the approach only works because of its focus. P&G advertises hundreds of brands, but each has a specific niche. Tide is a family-focused product that boasts stain-removing power. Ivory Snow is the gentler option, particularly crafted for babies' sensitive skin. Cheer is all about keeping colors bright. Gain is focused on fragrance. It's impossible for a single brand to cover all of these bases—engineers have yet to be able to develop a product that is gentle, removes stains, smells nice, and keeps colors bright. And customers intuitively understand this, which is why Procter & Gamble builds credibility by keeping each brand focused on a unique target and key benefit rather than squandering its credibility by pretending that every brand does everything well.

What's important to note, however, is that Procter & Gamble doesn't choose just one target, even though its strategy is one of focus. This is not a company that leaves money on the table. *It built a brand for every target.* P&G markets more than a dozen other detergent brands, each with its own focus and ideal customer. As a result, P&G has the entire market covered, but every customer is buying a product specifically crafted for them. Brilliant.

I know I'm preaching to the choir on this. Many funeral homes have at least one "off-brand" offering, probably a direct cremation or low-cost outlet in addition to the "flagship" brand. Some own a full lineup of a half-dozen or more ethnically, religiously, and/or demographically centered brands oriented toward a particular customer. Nonetheless, even the firms that are taking such an intentional, segmented approach often fail to capitalize on its full power, for two reasons: they either base their targets on the wrong factors or, in practice, fail to target at all.

Demographics alone make for a poor targeting strategy. This is vital to understand, and it goes against a widespread misunderstanding about targeted marketing.

We know that we could select three 55-year-old, middle-class, white women from the same city at random, and they will likely make very different decisions in terms of lifestyle and behavior. They might live in different parts of the city, be married to different types of men, vote for different political parties, and shop at different stores. One might home-school while another works full-time. One might feel strongly that the environment is the most pressing concern; one might not believe in climate change at all. In our personal interactions, we understand that it is insulting and wrong to assume that two people of the same sex, race, income, and age necessarily think alike. And yet, this understanding inexplicably disappears when we begin to talk about marketing. Demographic targeting assumes that all 55-year-old middle-class, white women have the same tastes. They don't.

Consider your low-cost option. You've likely said that it's targeted to low-income families. And yet, you've surely observed that many of your customers are not low-income at all, but instead somewhat affluent families who simply don't want to pay for an elaborate funeral (or any funeral at all). Meanwhile, many low-income families may be those who believe most firmly in the value of a funeral (perhaps for religious or cultural reasons that transcend affluence) and will therefore go to great lengths—pooling community resources, cashing in life savings, or asking extended family members to chip in—to pay for a full, traditional service. I once observed a young couple in an impoverished part of town walking up and down the street with a cardboard sign, soliciting donations from passing cars to pay for their relative's funeral.

Purchasing decisions, and the values behind them, defy demographic categories. People sometimes behave along demographic lines, but at best, this only explains *what* is happening, never *why*. The distinction is important if we want our marketing to work. Bobby Calder, Professor Emeritus of Marketing at the Kellogg School of Management, explains:

> Suppose we are in the food service business. We do a survey of a certain demographic group. We find that 85 percent of the consumers in this group have eaten chicken at least four times in the week surveyed… These consumers are chicken eaters!… Here is the problem: Where is the explanation? We could predict that these consumers would keep eating chicken (and therefore it should be a bigger part of our menu). But this is a prediction, not an explanation… Perhaps our consumers are concerned about their weight and are eating chicken to diet. Or maybe they are eating it to save money. With an explanation along either of these two lines, one could predict that, after accomplishing, or tiring, of their goal, consumers will no longer eat chicken.[1]

Demographic trends may (or may not) provide insight into what decisions people make, but we must go deeper if we wish to truly understand—and connect with—our customer. You might have built your targeting strategy on *demographic* assumptions, but people will react to the brand in *psychographic* ways. "Psychographics" simply means attitudes, aspirations, values, opinions, and lifestyles.[2] A disadvantaged family that can only afford a direct cremation and an affluent family that only wants a direct cremation have very little in common demographically, but they share a psychographic trait: they both desire to spend as little money as possible on a funeral.

Remarkably, even ethnically-targeted brands are, in reality, segmented more by psychographic needs than by demographics. Funeral directors have shared with me that as communities historically tied to particular ethnicities age and move into their second and third generations, successive generations are less likely to "stick with" the old brand. The younger generations share the same demographics as older generations, but their mindsets—the psychographics—change.

What to the first generation might have been a symbol of community and tradition is to a younger generation a tired symbol of the past. To one, community was defined by neighborhood and country of origin; to the other, community is defined by a digital circle of friends. Thus, ethnically targeted funeral homes are not in fact targeting by ethnicity at all; they are targeting the psychographic mindset *within* a given ethnicity that places value on particular cultural norms and traditions. Once that mindset changes, the brand connection is lost, even if the demographic variables remain constant.

Ethnicity and income aside, it's a tall order for a single brand to meet the needs of everyone in a city. Some people value face-to-face interaction, while others prefer to do everything online. Some are DIYers; others like to hire and delegate. Some consider their church the center of their community; others will draw community from a wide variety of interactions and places. Some have been to a dozen funerals this year; others have avoided funeral homes for decades. Each of these will have unique expectations and needs when they walk through your door, and if you want to be a successful brand, you need to do more than simply accommodate them. You need to convince them that you're *built for them.*

You must be not only the obvious choice, but the only choice.

What would the business model look like for a funeral home that was built not for a bargain-shopper, but for somebody who had been burned by traditional funeral homes in the past? I've seen extensive research confirming that there are plenty of these particular fish out there, and that they're viscerally driven to seek alternatives. Yet to my knowledge, nobody has gone after this seemingly easy target with any intentionality.

What about the DIYer? The popularity of shows like *Fixer Upper*, an explosion of YouTube how-to videos, and a growing interest in hobbies from urban farming to breadmaking have helped to facilitate an explosion of the do-it-yourself ethic. *The New York Times* catalogued one extreme version of DIY death-care, but we need not go so far as at-home body prep.[3] A growing percentage of cremation families prefer to organize, schedule, and plan the memorial service themselves. Funeral homes have yet to capitalize on even the mildest opportunity to equip and enable good self-guided funeral planning. Instead, they just figure they aren't their customer. But the right brand could position itself as a valuable resource, rather than an obstacle, for those wishing to plan a backyard celebration of life in a month rather than a mortuary-chapel funeral in two days.

How about the Nones? Funeral homes are built for the religious. They include chapels and pulpits, they function much like a church performing a Sunday morning service, and the somber formality of a funeral mirrors that of a mass. For those who have rejected these aspects of life, the traditional funeral home is inherently repellent. Token changes like removal of pews might help, but they don't go nearly far enough. In fact, they intentionally don't go far enough; funeral homes don't eliminate the other religious trappings for fear of alienating their more religious customers. But that's exactly the point of focus; if one brand caters to the religious and another to the Nones, both could be served with precision and excellence rather than compromising their experiences by forcing them to meet in the middle.

For such approaches to work, whether with the most pioneering new psychographic niche or even your basic direct-cremation outlet, a brand must stick to its target. But even a well-intentioned attempt to focus can end up as a failure when the focus is in name only and not in practice.

If you choose to offer a direct cremation brand, that means accepting the reality that your flagship brand must never conduct a direct cremation. Tide is meaningless if Ivory Snow is just as good at removing stains. If you choose a brand portfolio strategy, it is absolutely essential that you stick to your guns.

Yum! Brands is the parent company of fast food chains including Taco Bell, KFC, and Pizza Hut.[4] Its strategy only works by keeping the brands distinct. It's all the same company, but KFC won't sell you a bean burrito. Once in a while, you might see two of these brands doubled up in a single food-court kiosk, but even then they are co-branded—one menu on the left, another on the right. There is no Yum! Restaurant where you can get it all. If you could buy fried chicken at any Pizza Hut, it would detract not only from KFC's business but would also diminish Pizza Hut's credibility as a serious pizza restaurant able to contend against Domino's or my local favorite. Success for any brand means focus.

The number one byproduct of direct cremation storefronts is confusion. Families don't understand why the offering here costs a fraction of what the same offering costs over there. Employees don't understand why they're all selling the same products at different prices. And hospice workers drive families to the low-cost option as a "hack" to access the same products for better prices. And all of them are right.

The only way around this is to draw strict lines of demarcation between brands. You can't let your fried chicken joint sell bean burritos. If a family in your direct cremation shop wants to plan a small ceremony, that's not an opportunity to boost averages—it's proof of miscommunication. Refer them to your flagship brand where you can be certain they'll be better served. If a family in your main office decides they only want direct cremation, refer them to your low-cost provider where they can get the streamlined service they're looking for.

On the micro level, this seems harsh. How can a service brand turn away families? Why on earth would I make them drive all the way across town? But a business leader (and an effective servant) must think beyond the immediate moment. A company that tries to do everything can be effective at nothing. If you ask your main-brand funeral directors to do direct cremation, you're asking them to do something that contradicts their reason for showing up to work, and their primary work will inevitably suffer as a result. You want a direct-cremation provider to be efficient, fast, and no-frills, but you're going to hamstring his ability to be those things if you ask him to keep an extensive product list on hand, or train him on how to manage a service, "just in case." Focus breeds excellence, and both require discipline.

If a targeted approach makes sense for your firm, then you don't have to go out and launch three new businesses. The first step is to start taking targeting seriously through the brands you already offer. Be willing to turn families away. This will be easier if you can refer them to another of your own brands, but it's vital that you do so even if you can't recoup the revenue elsewhere. What's at stake is something more valuable than the lost case: it's the value of your brand, the only asset you own with the potential to continually grow in value. If you can instill discipline and focus, you're investing in a clear, differentiated, appreciating brand to which both employees and families will develop attachment and devotion.

That brings us to advertising, and an important question. Have you ever seen a Superbowl ad that featured the brand's CEO talking to the camera?

When you have something important to say, you say it in a way that's tailored to your audience. I would express my loyalty to my wife, to my sons, and to my business partners in three very different ways; I wouldn't try to tell them all at once. That's what makes brands like Old

Spice, Budweiser, and Nike so great at advertising. They decide ahead of time exactly who they are talking to, and then they talk to that person, instead of trying to talk to everybody. "Smell Like a Man, Man,"[5] "Whassup,"[6] and "Just Do It"[7] are carefully refined messages designed to engage a specific target. As a result, the message is delivered with clarity, and their target audience hears it and knows it's for them.

As business categories evolve, their advertising tends to do so as well. This is why turn-of-the-century advertising often feels so quaint and charming. The descriptions were detailed but simplistic because the product itself was a novelty. To sell refrigerators or perfume to an audience that hadn't previously had access to such luxuries required little more than a product description. A 1906 ad for an automobile shows only a photo of the car and paragraphs upon paragraphs describing its features. More than a century later, the category has grown far more sophisticated, and competition for a car buyer's attention has grown far more intense. As a result, car brands have succeeded through careful positioning.

Ford's Trucks division chose to focus on a single psychographic characteristic to define its target audience. "Built Ford Tough" has helped solidify the F-series' position as the best-selling vehicle in the world.[8] Toyota invested heavily in positioning the Prius as synonymous with environmentally responsible efficiency. As a result, the brand dominates market share, consistently beating out a growing range of other hybrid competitors.[9] If you want to make a statement that you care about the environment, Prius is an obvious choice. Meanwhile, Tesla carved out a niche for itself within an already crowded luxury market by positioning its vehicles as a statement on modernity and innovation against a category steeped in tradition and conservatism (think Mercedes-Benz or Cadillac).

None of these brands want everybody. They all decided exactly who they would target, and they go after that target audience with a laser focus. Tesla succeeds by pricing itself out of competition with Prius. Prius succeeds by advertising exactly the features an F-150 owner would detest. If you drive an F-150, you probably poke fun at the snooty design of Tesla trucks. But these brands don't care about who they're losing because of the devotees they're too busy winning. All of them succeed by becoming a part of their customer's identity, making bold declarations about themselves as well as their customers. To purchase a vehicle is as much a statement about yourself as it is an investment in transportation.

Meanwhile, funeral advertising has stayed far behind the curve. The industry norm is for an owner or funeral director to be talking to the camera on TV, or portraited in a suit and tie for a print ad, accompanied by a scripty font and vague sentiments about family, dignity, and care. Not only is one local competitor impossible to tell apart from another, the message is as forgettable as it is formulaic.

Such advertising is expected to speak to everybody, which blurs the message and its impact. And with little innovation or differentiation in the substance of the business—with every competitor and every brand offering the same lineup of products and services—it can feel like there's little to talk about with any specificity. These are all good reasons why mortuary marketing remains weak. But they don't change the fact that your advertising dollars are largely being wasted.

The pressure to stick with industry conventions creates a rare opportunity for funeral homes. In the insurance business, "going negative" was taboo until 2010—insurance companies sold *assurance*, never dreaming of alluding to the disaster from which they shielded you. That is, until Allstate shattered the norm with "Mayhem." The campaign didn't just feature the chaos that could ensue with the wrong insurance, it personified it and made it into a recurring antihero character.[10] The campaign was a roaring success that helped Allstate pull ahead of its competition. Within two quarters of Mayhem's launch, Allstate saw sales increase by 4.3 percent (a colossal gain in an industry measured at the margins).[11]

While its competitors were sticking to safer (albeit humorous) spots about trust and saving money, Allstate was blowing them out of the water by speaking straight to its audience about worst-case scenarios.

A TV campaign highlighting all the ways a cheap funeral could end up a disaster is probably not the way for you to go. But your business exists within a field where even a small dose of courage and creativity in advertising could put you miles ahead of your competition. In a market where everybody is saying and doing the same thing, the slightest difference can make the greatest impact.

Consider, too, that Mayhem avoided broad appeal at every turn. Part of the reason the ads were so successful is that they were incredibly specific for their category. One ad centers around a cat-induced flood.[12] Another introduces an exasperated teenage girl committing a hit-and-run while texting and driving.[13] Another talks to homeowners about the high costs of raccoon damage.[14] Obviously, Allstate sold to more people than cat owners, parents of teenagers, and homeowners in raccoon country, but the focus of each ad allowed its spokescharacter to talk about something of substance.

I can imagine someone at Allstate saying, "But we want to sell insurance to parents of male teenagers, too! Can we add a boy to the spot? And what about loss from other rodents? We don't want people to think we can't help with squirrel damage!" This kind of thinking kills good advertising. If you're going after everybody, empty tropes will be all you have to talk about. The more specific you're willing to be in your marketing, the more meaningful your message will be. You may be pleasantly surprised. Even those who fall outside your net will often be attracted to your confidence and clarity.

That kind of specificity is hard to achieve when you're the star of the ad. Mayhem (like any great campaign) works to shift the focus *off* of Allstate. In Budweiser's "Whassup," the main characters *are* the Budweiser target audience. In Old Spice's "Smell Like a Man, Man," the spokesman initiates a playful conversation with the consumer and the woman in his life *about* the consumer. "Just Do It" is a message of motivation that equates the athlete in us all with the sports legends of history. Nike rarely showcases its products, designers, or executives in its ads; instead it positions legendary athletic achievement in such a way as to help you see yourself in the shoes of your heroes.

In Coca Cola's advertising, Coke is usually a guest at the party where you're the host (even going so far as to print your name on its product).[15] Procter & Gamble's Always brand celebrated its target's feminine strength with #LikeAGirl.[16] The Most Interesting Man in the World even had the audacity to push his product out of the limelight, saying, "I *don't always* drink beer, but when I do, I *prefer* Dos Equis."[17] A self-absorbed beer ad would include a pitchman who *always* drinks beer, and *always* chooses Dos Equis. The campaign's magnanimity is its genius.

Good branding (like a good funeral director) focuses on the customer. And you can't do that when the camera is literally focused on you. Nor can you do it when you haven't decided to which customer you want to speak.

Consider your website. It's incredible how much content on the average mortuary website is about the mortuary: "Our Story," "About Us," "Why Choose Us," "Why We're Different," "Meet Our Team," "How We Work," "Our Services." A homepage might feature the owner's photograph, his grandfather's photograph, a note from him, an image of his signature, a link to "read more" about him, and a list of awards presented to his company by local associations. Only the very worst funeral guest would talk so much about himself in the presence of a grieving family. A funeral director who did so would be fired. Not only are your family heritage and accolades uninteresting to a bereaved and disoriented family, they could be taken as evidence that you're more interested in yourself than in them.

This kind of marketing goes wrong because its objective is wrong. You might think the aim of good marketing is to get more leads. This may be true, but that must be secondary to a more important goal: you need to get more of the *right* leads. This is important for two reasons. First, focusing on the right leads will improve your marketing because it will make it more effective (focus beats blurry every time). Second, it will also yield greater ROI on the sales side, because your associates won't have to work as hard to sell to leads that your marketing has already engaged and prequalified. If you want to go after no-frills, middle-of-the-road customers, then you need a streamlined, utilitarian GPL; streamlined, utilitarian promises in your advertising; and streamlined, utilitarian funeral directors. Building a straight road requires getting everything lined up in advance, but it's a lot easier to drive than one full of hairpin turns.

If you're marketing to everybody, then you'll resonate strongly with nobody, and come off as self-centered—not because you are, but because *you* are the only topic you can discuss with any meaningful specificity. But if you're marketing to a precise target, they will understand that you know them and love them before they even walk in the door. The people you want will be drawn to you, and those who you don't will intuitively understand that they'll be better served elsewhere (hopefully by another brand that you own).

More than one mortuary owner has described his strategy to me like this: "I roll everything I can under my parent brand, because that's the name people know. I'd have to spend a lot more in advertising to get people to recognize other brand names."

The problem with that approach is it's designed around what's easiest for the brand—not what's easiest for the customer. They're right about one thing: advertising a single brand is a lot more *efficient*. But for a commoditized business category like death care, it's far less *effective*. Familiarity isn't the same thing as devotion; very few of the people you know would give up a Saturday to help you move. So while an entire town might *know* your flagship brand, the majority of them might think of it as too expensive, too traditional, too mainstream, or too fancy for their tastes. That's why good ad tracking research will measure not one, but two variables: awareness and preference. Those who know you and those who love you are two very different groups.

If you can build a brand that clearly plants a flag and says, "This is who we serve," then you can build your product and service offerings around that person. Then you can market confidently and clearly to her, saying, "We exist for you." And when she walks into your office, your sales team will have the luxury of selling with confidence, providing exactly what she is looking for. Because you've already told her that's what she can expect from you.

In my part of the country, we have clothing stores that sell western and workwear clothing. Their marketing is specific and focused. Their radio ads never boast about having "something for everyone"; instead they focus on a blue-collar, rural audience. If you need pearl-snaps and cowboy hats, they've got you covered. If you need wingtips and khakis, you can go somewhere else.

The result is twofold. If I'm looking for a new pair of boots, I have a higher expectation that this place will have exactly what I need. I expect their staff to be experts on work boots, and I expect them to have a better selection than a generic department store. So, when I need work boots, that's where I'm going. But I also have lower expectations that they'll be able to help me in other areas. If I want to buy dress shoes and a tie, their sales staff is under no pressure to try to accommodate me, and I'm not going to be surprised when they don't.

That's why focused branding is good for your sales efforts. It allows your team to be expert leaders rather than reactionary followers. The pride, confidence, and fulfillment that comes from this difference is of great value to your firm, because happier people do better work. Business seminars, books, and articles abound extolling the legendary virtues of an empowered, engaged sales staff like those of Zappos[18] or Ritz Carlton.[19] But it's impossible to reach those heights if you're expecting your staff to appease anybody who walks in the door. Ritz Carlton staff will only ever serve a tiny fraction of the population—and them only during specific moments. Zappos is focused on footwear—and footwear for people who shop online specifically. "All things to all people" is antithetical to the expertise and quality your customers and employees want you to provide.

But if your team knows what they do and who they do it for, then they also know what they don't do and who they don't do it for. They don't have to waste time or energy trying to force it. Imagine telling a frustrated funeral director that he never has to do direct cremations again. Or telling the staff at your low-cost storefront that they will never have to plan a service again. Their relief and elation will pay dividends for you the next time they sit down to do the job they *want* to do.

Likely, you invest heavily in training and improving your arrangements processes: checking monthly analytics, watching video playbacks, and considering sales product by product. I've never met an owner who can't tell me who his best and worst funeral directors are, by the numbers, off the top of his head. But all of this attention places an extraordinary amount of pressure on a single meeting with a family. You feel the strain, and so do your staff and those you're trying to serve. All of your eggs are in the basket of a tightly choreographed series of decisions made by a family at the worst possible moment, often (for them) in the worst possible setting.

This only exacerbates other challenges in your business. For example, good help is hard to find, particularly in funeral service. I have yet to talk to a mortuary owner who says it's easy to hire good funeral directors. Nonetheless, whatever funeral directors you have are in the hot seat every single time they're sitting across from a family. They know this is only one of a few at-bats they'll get, and they have to carry the team. And you know that you might not have the roster needed to win the game. An undue focus on sales, case counts, and contract averages piles additional pressure on top of an already weak pressure point.

That's why marketing is so important. Engineers alleviate excessive strain on a single point by spreading the weight across a wider base.

Consider if the burden of the arrangement process could be spread over years of interaction with the family. Good brand marketing introduces who you are with confidence and specificity, rather than just saying that you exist (or that you care, which is the same thing). You can't expect it to yield results the next day—that's not what it's for. The purpose is that your customer can devote a tiny fraction of her mental energy to deciding whether or not she likes you long before the tumult of the at-need moment.

Over time, and with continued exposure, that decision strengthens into outright preference (rather than awareness alone) for your brand. When a death occurs, she might look at a few websites, but you're already at the top of the stack in her mind. A review of your website confirms her good opinion. She sees products and services that look like they're built for her. "People like us use a funeral home like this," she thinks.

By the time she walks into your funeral home, the sale is as good as done. She already understands who you are and why you're a fit. Your team recognizes that she's a fit; she's looking for what they exist to provide. Everyone is more predisposed to a favorable review of the process because everyone is doing what they want to do—nothing is being stretched or strained.

But this only works if you're focused on *her*. A billboard photo of three generations of your family will never build this kind of affinity. Your marketing must prove, specifically, how you cater to your target audience, which means first choosing a target audience and then building your business around it, so that you can equip your funeral directors to recognize and become experts on serving that target audience.

This approach is a growth strategy if you're managing a portfolio of multiple brands across your company, segmented by various targets' specific needs, attitudes, perceptions, and desires. It can be particularly confidence-boosting for a brand to turn away a customer if they're doing so to refer them to a better-suited sister brand—after all, the family will be happier and the money's all ending up in the same place.

But if your size or resources preclude a diversified portfolio approach, it's still important to understand that a focused, confident brand beats a generic, desperate one every time. It's a fallacy to assume that by focusing your market, you shrink your market. Ferrari has seen success by historically limiting the number of cars it sells so that it can protect the "dream of exclusivity."[20] That lets Ferrari charge far more per vehicle (and collect far greater margins) than its more broad-based competitors. Costco won't let non-members into its store, a strategy that has helped it more than hurt it and created an entire revenue line through membership sales that its competitors will never have.[21]

If you can only afford to adopt a focused strategy for a single brand, and if every family you turn away goes to a competitor, you can still grow and succeed. Because for the family that matches your focus, sales will come easier, satisfaction will be greater, and your services will be better. Others will still trickle in, just like Mountain Dew targets hyperactive 22-year-old males but may occasionally sell a soda to a 55-year-old woman. But for your target, you will stop being one choice among many and will instead become the obvious choice.

When you think about it, growth (especially when measured by caseload) is an arbitrary objective. Is having more cases really the best measure of success? More staff to pay? More calls in the middle of the night? For many firms, case counts are an unhelpful distraction and drive decision-making toward desperate, undisciplined moves. If your firm was doing a better job (as measured by both satisfaction and revenue) of serving fewer people, it's worth considering what your life might look like in that scenario, as opposed to more cases of grab-bag variety. McDonald's has sold more cheeseburgers than In-N-Out[22] but will never come close to the latter's zealous fan base, nor its per-transaction profitability.[23] Which brand is more successful? It depends on how you define success.

Chances are you didn't get into this business to become the leading national funeral home. A little competitive spirit is great. Big numbers feel good. There's something gratifying about having the biggest market share in town, but there's something even more gratifying about being the best at serving families (and likely the most profitable doing so). Usually, that requires some decisions about whom you exist to serve.

Many of the compromises you feel pressured to make along the way may paradoxically be compromising your ability to serve and lead families like you want to—and they might even be costing you money. Somewhere out there is a family that needs exactly the style and expertise that you are best equipped to provide. If you can find them, tell them, and then show them that they're exactly whom you're here for, they will love you for it. They will probably be willing to pay you more for it. And you will have taken the first steps toward building a brand that is confident, focused, and positioned to both lead and serve the families who need you most.

Chapter 10
How We Make Money

Not many morticians have experience in construction, but the two industries are uniquely analogous.

If you've ever hired a general contractor—perhaps to build a new location—chances are you were happiest with the company at the outset of the project. This is where general contractors have the most opportunity to provide value. Their knowledge of buildings, permitting, codes, zoning, schedules, and the overall process can provide great assurance and peace of mind to a bewildered and disoriented client. A good one can look at a draft set of plans and suggest modifications that the architect might not have considered—a cost-saving measure here, or an end-use improvement there. But you don't pay for any of these services. They're freebies provided up front in hopes of securing the contract.

Similarly, think about the end of the project. Sometimes after the grand opening is when you need a contractor the most. There's always a punch list, and some general contractors will occasionally do "warranty" work after the job is complete. You may even wish to move a door or change a paint color that you hadn't thought through as well at the planning stage. But this type of work isn't something in a contractor's budget. It represents a drain on whatever profit they may have made on the job. After the ribbon-cutting, contractors hope that you don't call them—at exactly the moment you wish you had them on speed dial.

But in the middle of the project, when they're really doing what you hired them to do, is ironically when your satisfaction, expectations, and attention to the project are all at their lowest. The complexity of the work invariably causes delays, surprise costs pop up where you least expect, and as the work drags on you are often asked to make compromises or sacrifice time, money, features, or all of the above.

What's interesting is that the moments in which you value a general contractor most are when you're paying them least, and vice versa. Before the project gets underway, a contractor is essentially working for free— giving away their hard-earned expertise as an unpaid consultant in hopes of winning the project. And at the end, the finishing touches and tiny details that are so important to you are just an unaccounted-for burden to your contractor. Strangely, the project itself is the lowest-value and the thinnest-margin part of the work.

Morticians and general contractors have a lot in common. Competition is tight, price-shopping abounds, and if you do your job right, you've hidden from the customer the very complexity that they're paying you for, so they never really understand nor appreciate your value.

Acer, the Taiwanese computing hardware company, developed the concept of the "smiling curve" to describe this phenomenon in the 1990s.[1] The curve represents perceived customer value at various phases of the business process, from concept to sale. As a manufacturer, the vast majority of Acer's overhead and costs went into the fabrication of a product— unsurprising for a manufacturing company. But what founder Stan Shih recognized was that manufacturing is actually the area of the *least* value (the middle of the curve). What customers really value is the *concept,* on the left-hand side of the curve, and the marketing or articulation of value, on the right-hand side.

FIGURE 10.1: THE SMILING CURVE

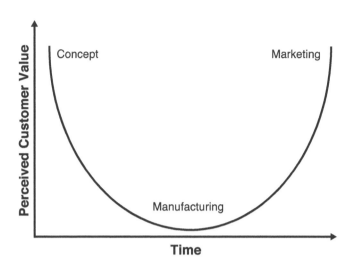

Acer once thought of itself as a manufacturing company. But Shih helped the company understand that its innovations and marketing were of far greater value to customers—the former to solve their problem and the latter to help them cut through the clutter of available options and better understand how Acer could help. The manufacturing was the delivery mechanism, but it provided minimal opportunity to differentiate or prove value to the customer.

While the customer's perceived value can be plotted as a smiling curve, many industries (including construction and death care) tend to deliver on a "frowning" curve," concentrating on the lowest-value products and services on the spectrum, while giving away or neglecting the high-value opportunities.[2]

FIGURE 10.2: CONSTRUCTION'S FROWNING CURVE

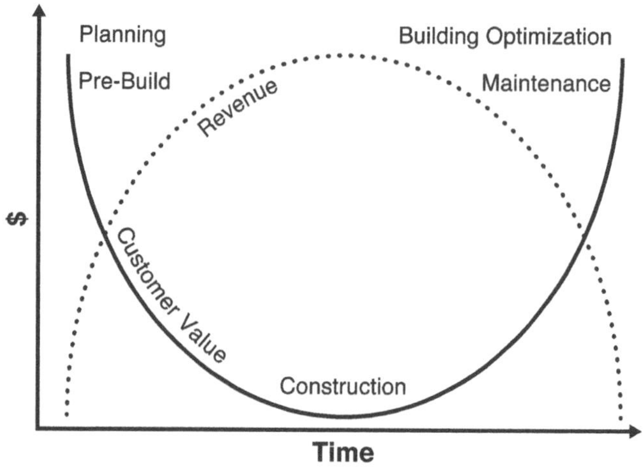

Apple presents a great example of a company that uses this concept to its advantage. Few iPhone users know anything about how a smartphone is made—and if Apple changed its production process, customers wouldn't care. What sets Apple apart is its ability to connect its concept to its customer—something a brand can only do when it focuses on the things its customer values.

Anybody can manufacture the iPhone—other companies manufactured smartphones before Apple did. In fact, the design isn't even that special; design was simply the nuts and bolts of how to deliver on Apple's insights. But amidst a pile of failed smartphones, the iPhone succeeded. Why? Competitors talked about features, design processes, and data capacity, while Apple was demonstrating how the concept would change your life. And from its sleek packaging to the ultramodern stores in which it was sold, Apple concentrated on the parts of the process that customers could understand and appreciate.

Three years after the release of the iPhone, ads for Microsoft's Windows Phone emphasized the making of the product. One TV commercial ends with a statement describing the decisions Microsoft made "when we set out to make a smartphone..."[3] Another describes the product as "*designed* to get you in, and out, and back to life."[4] There's a self-congratulating air to the whole campaign. In both ads, the software company compares its product to the design decisions of its competitors, and explains how it did it better. At least Microsoft rose above a list of product features. But it couldn't resist the urge to talk about itself: its product, its design process, and its motivations. Microsoft's designers wanted to bring the customer into their office and tell them all about how they'd made this thing. But nobody except Microsoft's designers cared. Windows Phone never even achieved 4 percent of market share.[5]

The same year, Apple ran an ad introducing its FaceTime app in the iPhone 4.[6] There's no voiceover detailing Apple's design process. In fact, there's no voiceover at all. The ad is just a tear-jerking compilation of people using FaceTime to transform their lives: a couple communicating long-distance using sign language (presumably for the first time), a father on a business trip smiling at his toddler and wife at home, elderly grandparents waving at a granddaughter in her cap and gown, a deployed soldier watching an ultrasound of his baby. Within two quarters, Apple commanded an unprecedented 29.5 percent of the burgeoning smartphone market.[7] No other competitor came close.

Microsoft talked about itself and the design decisions that *it* cared about. But Apple showed how it could dramatically enrich the parts of your life that *you* care about.

Brands like Microsoft and industries like construction leave money on the table by focusing on the wrong part of the smiling curve. But there's an even bigger danger. Monetizing the wrong part of your business, or misunderstanding where your value really lies with customers, can create misaligned incentives that actually push customers further away.

In my own line of work, hourly billing was the norm for decades. I spent days out of every month totaling up the hours my staff and I had spent, client by client, project by project, and reconciling those numbers against client-specific rates and estimates before we could send out our bills. For some clients, those invoices included an attachment breaking down (in six-minute increments) all of the work that justified their bill.

But every month, I couldn't shake the feeling that this was all wrong. Clients didn't want our time; they wanted their marketing to work. They might understand paying $1,000 for our insight, but it was tougher to explain paying $50 for a 15-minute phone call. Consciously or unconsciously, the incentives were driving a wedge between us; we would make more money if a project took longer (regardless of whether it was successful), and every bill taught our clients (wrongly) to value our time more than our efficacy.

We went to great lengths to protect our transparency, accountability, and honesty so that we never took advantage of clients, but at some point it just didn't matter; our incentives were misaligned and everybody knew it. When an important meeting justified four or five key staff members, I could see the client cringing, as if they were adding up the dollar signs floating above our heads.

So, we spent years overhauling our billing process to better align incentives. This was completely heretical in our business. Internally, some worried that we wouldn't be able to gauge profitability or make informed decisions about how to allocate resources. Our peers at other firms told us we were crazy; they wished they could abandon timesheets, they said, but had become convinced that it was impossible.

Still, we ate the elephant one bite at a time. For a few production-oriented clients, we set up menus with a points structure. For others we shifted to project fees; we would simply deliver what we promised for a set fee, but we would only receive our full fee upon completion. Other clients were a good fit for retainers; they'd pay us the same amount each month, and we worried about fluctuating volume for them. Some clients have even worked on performance-based models where we only get paid if our work is successful. All of this incentivized us to work faster and smarter so that clients didn't have to wait as long. It also helped us to spend less time counting minutes and more time focused on client needs. Clients have recognized that and appreciate the alignment; what is good for us is now good for them, too.

In early 2020, just weeks before the COVID-19 outbreak forced us to begin working from home, we converted our last legacy client away from hourly billing and held a staff meeting in which we all tore up our timesheets to celebrate. The timing couldn't have been better; when COVID inflicted its economic turmoil, we were able to operate with laser focus on what was best for our clients, never distracted by having to tally up billable hours. I'm convinced that the shift of approach made a life-or-death difference during a crucial period for our company.

For a funeral home, it's even more important to align your incentives with your families than it is for other businesses. In Chapter 7 we discussed "the gap"—the unfair, disadvantaged starting point of the funeral home. Incentives are already almost insurmountably misaligned. The family knows that you are profiting from one of their worst days. There's little that can be done to change that fact; unless people stop dying, or unless funeral homes become nonprofits (neither is a likely scenario), "the gap" will always be your reality.

As a result, it's absolutely vital to do everything you can to mitigate this challenge—recognizing, minimizing, and managing the gap, and never widening it. This can be a difficult task. Death-as-business is the water in which you're swimming, so it can be almost impossible for you to identify places where the family might perceive a misalignment. You know that charging for this or that service is standard industry practice. But to the families you serve, it might be one more line item they don't understand—or worse, one more place they suspect you're taking advantage of them during their moment of need.

If we apply the concept of the smiling curve to funeral service, it might look something like this:

FIGURE 10.3: DEATH CARE'S SMILING CURVE

At the very center of the curve is merchandise: that which families need least, value least, and suspect most. As we move outward in either direction, we begin to identify the value funeral homes offer in the overall process: on the left, the reassurance that comes from planning and your expertise, and on the right, the relief of not having to coordinate with a pastor, build a slideshow, or worry about the details of publishing an obituary.

Working our way up the curve, of even greater value is the reassurance of the first call and the clarity and guidance that a funeral home can provide within only a few moments of the death. And the actual disposition of the body remains high-value because, to date, this is something families are largely unable to handle on their own and is, in their own perception, one of your chief roles.

The center of the curve captures the spectrum of traditional funeral service: all of the products and services offered within the tiny window of a few days wherein the funeral director does his job. But if we look further up the curve, on the left we see even greater value conferred through preplanning, which offers all the benefits of at-need arrangements *plus* the satisfaction and assurance of having provided for one's survivors. And on the right, long after the funeral occurs, aftercare and long-term grief resources present a high-value opportunity to serve families that is often either neglected or underappreciated by the funeral home.

It's important to note that as we move further up the curve in either direction, the gap—the misalignment of incentives between your interests and the family's—diminishes, because the emotion and vulnerability of grief is inherently lower the further people are from the moment of loss. Therefore, there is a double benefit for funeral homes that look outward and upward on the curve. Not only does doing so confer the benefit of greater perceived value (as in most industries), it also helps steer clear of the moment at which you are most vulnerable to suspicion and misunderstanding.

We've already discussed in some detail how merchandise sales are a liability when families are predisposed to mistrust the industry. Funeral homes have been steadily losing trust in the public's eye since 1963,[8] and their attempts to make up for the accompanying loss of revenue have compounded the problem. Product sales have been a stopgap to make some extra money, but they've continued to erode the trust of the public by proving (in their minds) that funeral directors are exactly the slick salesmen families suspect them to be.

For years, I've dreamed of the possibility of a funeral home that offers products at cost. It would be a staggeringly powerful statement (in no small part because it would require a substantial sacrifice on the part of the funeral home). But that's exactly the power of such an idea. The grand gesture of leaving money on the table in the service of one's clients could pay dividends in public attention and trust. It wouldn't be impossible, in fact, for the additional market share and confidence gained from such a move to more than offset the losses in revenue.

These kinds of gains have a precedent in other industries. As my firm has moved toward retainers and project fees for our clients, billing on a service-based model, we have stopped marking up many goods and third-party services we purchase on behalf of clients. Again, we don't want to be incentivized to upsell. If we make the same amount of money regardless, then clients trust us more (and often spend more).

Honoraria and other passthrough costs have long been common in funeral service; not everything is an opportunity to make a buck. By simply shifting that needle further to one side, funeral homes can say, "This isn't the core of our business, and therefore it's not where we make our money." In doing so, they have an opportunity to regain public trust—and zoom past competitors in the process. Obviously, such a move would require extensive planning and cost-benefit analysis, but the fact that it's never been done shouldn't be a deterrent on its own.

Merchandise is one way to recoup lost revenue, but as we've seen, it's one for which funeral homes pay dearly. Still, it represents only a single point on the smiling curve. A careful consideration of every point on the curve will help the industry better match up its revenue model and offerings with the family's needs and expectations. Funeral homes have numerous opportunities to better align incentives and focus on the points that convey the greatest value, rather than selling a "frowning" curve by charging the most for the products and services the family values least.

Consider preneed sales. In my firm's extensive research on death care, I've heard a lot of confusing—and often contradictory—reasons to preplan. Do it to keep your kids from screwing up your funeral. Do it to save money. Do it for peace of mind. Do it for the free food we'll give you to listen to our pitch.

Most of these flunk the smell test. "What do I care what my funeral is like? I'd rather spend that money on something I can enjoy. And I thought you just told me funerals are for the living... so shouldn't I be okay if my kids need a different funeral than what I would have planned?" Then comes the death blow: "Besides, I don't have to worry about that. I told my kids to just cremate me and stick my ashes in a coffee can."

It's amazing how appeals to frugality, clarity, or peace of mind fall apart in the face of an empty can of Folger's. It's because even the best preneed pitches are focused on the wrong point of the smiling curve.

Consider the vast resources you devote upfront to selling, years and sometimes decades in advance, the very products and services that are at the low-value center of the curve. The products your preneed sales team are selling are the same as those your at-need associates are selling. You charge for them the same way, you present them the same way, and you profit from them in largely the same way. But the perceived value of the transaction is completely different. People make preneed arrangements driven by different motivations, in a different state of mind, for a different recipient, and with a different payment structure than they do at-need. Preplanning also has a smaller "gap" since you're not meeting the customer during a moment of grief and confusion. Why, then, should preplanning be monetized so similarly to at-need?

A funeral home that (for example) charged a flat fee to preplan would be making a statement: "Our planning services alone have value. You're not just buying funeral service sans inflation; you're actually buying a gift for your survivors." The current sales model teaches advance-planning clients that what you're selling won't have value until they pass away, because that's when they'll receive the goods you're charging for and you'll make your money.

Charging an initial fee to indicate that the real value is in the consultative expertise of your advance planning team would shift the transaction to the left on the smiling curve. They'd pay sticker price for the funeral, of course. But they wouldn't have to wait until they die to receive the true *value* of preplanning—the peace of mind, clarity, and knowledge that they've blessed their children from beyond the grave. They'd get to enjoy all of that today, and your fee structure would reinforce that value.

Instead, funeral homes currently give away what consumers perceive as high value as a means to sell more of the low-value services at the middle of the curve. In fact, if inflation is worse than anticipated, you may even be selling the low-value middle at a loss. This is a poor use of the rare opportunity that a preplanning meeting affords to provide expert assurance. You're giving families clarity, guidance, assurance, and education that can only come from your expertise—arguably the most valuable asset you own. If you're giving that away for free, you're focusing on the wrong part of the transaction.

Or consider an exchange a bit closer to the time of need. The first call is arguably the moment when the funeral home offers the greatest value to the family. It is at this moment that you have the most emotionally-powerful opportunity to communicate your compassion and expertise, provide support and guidance, begin answering the questions the family needs answers to, and position your firm as the trustworthy expert that can shepherd them through the chaos ahead. But this moment is usually handled by the least-experienced, lowest-paid, and least-expert staff available.

That's not necessarily to say that you need to charge families for the first call, or tie your best funeral director to the front desk awaiting the next call. But treating that call as a valuable exchange in and of itself, rather than only a means to subsequent interaction, matters. Doing so would not only help to bolster the expertise and quality with which these calls are treated, it would also take the pressure to "make the sale" out of the equation so that you could start by *serving* rather than by *selling*.

Business consultant Patrick Lencioni calls this the "Getting Naked" approach. Outstanding service businesses, Lencioni writes, "avoid, as much as possible, telling clients what they would do if they were to be hired; instead they just start serving them as though they were already a client."[9] By stripping away the fear of losing the business, you can actually win it by jumping right in to help the family. There is no such thing as a "shopper"; there are only families in need of your service.

One offering that many funeral homes already provide is free removal. Families expect to get hit with costs and fees from the moment a funeral home gets involved. Those firms that offer free removal take the immediate pressure off of the distraught family—and rarely lose the business after the fact. Free care (storage) and transportation if a family changes its mind take it a step further, making the first decision completely risk-free for the family and putting some of the mortuary's skin in the game. This enables the funeral home to be perceived as trusted confidant rather than sale-seeking opportunist.

I'm always surprised when this offering is not consistently promoted, even when it is available. You might know that you're not going to charge, but families don't. I can't think of any more reassuring words at that moment than, "Mr. Layer, the only thing we really need to take care of right now is this: by state law you only have 24 hours to make a decision on what to do with your father's remains. We believe that's too fast to make a decision, so we'll bring him into our care completely free of charge while you decide what to do next. If you opt to use another funeral home, we'll transport him there free of charge as well."

That's leadership. Funeral homes should be shouting that kind of message from the rooftops. It's reassuring to have a difficult conversation with someone who is not only telling me what I need to be worried about but is doing the worrying for me.

If you believe in a right way, and if you believe that you're best equipped to care for the family, then the first call isn't about making a pitch, and it's not even about answering questions. It's about serving. It's about *proving* your service from the earliest possible moment, and looking for opportunities to provide whatever the family needs. You might ultimately make money the same way you always have, or you might find some new revenue opportunities. But the important thing is to not be *selling* at the moment you could be *serving*.

This mindset also applies at the other end of the curve, after the funeral has taken place, in an often-neglected pair of services: aftercare and grief support.

If funeral directors are to invest in guiding and leading families toward healthy grief (as opposed to simply selling the trappings of a traditional funeral), that decision implies a responsibility to aid in the grief process, which obviously lasts long after the funeral is over. Grief support is often connected to larger funeral homes through a nonprofit arm or community relationships, but it's usually treated as a side project with little serious investment. This is a missed opportunity to prove genuine value to families in a context divorced from the chaos and pressure of the death itself.

That's not to say that grief therapy must be sold as a product for a few hundred dollars a session. There are numerous revenue models that can be used. The important thing (as with any of these opportunities) is to match your investment in the service with the value conferred upon it by the family.

For example, many industries include warranties or long-term service contracts as part of the sale, and a funeral home that provides access to vetted, professional care and support as a benefit of funeral planning might easily command a premium. But doing so requires real investment; families can tell the difference between professional offerings and jury-rigged half-measures. A funeral home willing to invest in quality grief counseling (perhaps even hiring a staff psychiatrist) may incur extra cost, but would set itself head and shoulders above its competitors in terms of its genuineness and quality of care.

Aftercare, too, grows in value as the complexity of life, and therefore of death, multiplies. Death certificates, life insurance policies, and public notification decisions have always fallen tangentially within the purview of the funeral director. On reflection, it's somewhat arbitrary that social media accounts, banking, and federal programs would be any different. Some funeral homes have created guide sheets or lists to help families navigate aftercare needs. This is a step in the right direction, but it's still a wasted opportunity.

Funeral homes invest heavily in large display rooms and choreographed sales processes for a product the family distrusts and will only ever see for a couple of hours. Why, then, should the pressing practical problems that every family will have to navigate after a death be relegated to a single sheet of instructions that's given away for free? The value the customer places on an offering should match the emphasis you place on it.

A funeral home might keep a CPA or an attorney on staff—or at least on retainer—to assist with aftercare decisions. Or it might provide classes and resources to help families manage administrative needs, both before and after death. The idea is simply to broaden your focus to think through everything the family is worried about, positioning yourself as a responsive, helpful resource.

Yet another opportunity is showing up on the edges of the smiling curve that hasn't been there before. The decision of where, when, and how to finally lay the remains to rest is delayed later and later after death— both a blessing and a curse for the industry.

One of the interesting byproducts of an increasingly cremation-centric culture is the expansion of the period between death and the final laying to rest of the body. If not cremated, a body must be buried or entombed within a very short window of time. But as cremation grows in prevalence, families are becoming increasingly comfortable with the idea of deferring the final step for months or even years. A funeral professional might be well aware of the benefits of a final resting place, but increasingly, families are choosing to learn that lesson the hard way. That is creating a demand long after the death occurs for products and services historically tethered to the week of the passing. But it's a demand many in death care still aren't equipped to meet, and that families are rarely able to articulate.

Scatter Day was a big success because it created an altogether new product: the tradition of laying someone to rest within a nontraditional window of time. It wasn't the *cost* of a scattering or entombment that kept remains in closets; it was the *taboo* of not knowing what to do with them. In their grief, people have seized a novel opportunity to postpone the final farewell, but nobody has considered how to revisit the question later on. Families that decide against an immediate disposition can unknowingly lock themselves into a prison of deferred grief; companies that reconsider the what and when of final disposition can seize on a high-value opportunity to provide them an escape.

Self-styled "home death-care guide" Carol Boucher observes the growing importance of the length of the grieving process: "Virtually everyone who has had a conventional funeral and later comes to me says that they wish they had more time."[10] It's an intriguing concept. We can have food delivered to our door when we want it, an endless stream of movies on demand, and just about any product delivered overnight without us ever having to leave our homes. In this instant culture, we're all trained by experience that we can live life on our terms and according to own time frame.

Cremation confers the practical ability to choose with far greater flexibility the time and place of a final ceremony, scattering, burial, or entombment. The practical constraints that have historically limited this decision are hardly relevant at all today. A body is large, cumbersome, and comes with an intrinsically limited shelf life. Cremation transforms it into something conveniently portable and indefinitely storable.

As families increasingly choose cremation, and increasingly expect to deal with death in their own time frames, determining a final resting place slides to the right on the timeline and moves up the curve in terms of value. What used to be simply the last or second-to-last event in a compact week—or even day—of grief ceremonies (viewing, funeral, graveside, reception) now becomes a final step of letting go whenever the family is ready. That may be a month after the funeral is over, or it may be two decades.

None of this is to say that deferring this step in the process is the *right* decision for a family, but it may become yet another hill upon which funeral directors can decide whether to die or plant a flag. As families' grief processes lengthen, the window of time within which funeral homes may be of service opens ever wider. And there is a growing need for guidance in healthy grieving at a time other than the actual moment of death.

None of these opportunities may be exactly what your community needs or what your firm is set to deliver. Or they all might be. They're provided here only as thought starters and examples. Adjustments to your business model must be specific and intentional. They might not even be needs that families can articulate—designing based on polls or focus groups is a path fraught with danger, and Apple, Amazon, and other successful brands have famously succeeded by offering products and services customers could never have imagined. As Sony Founder Akio Morita once said, "Our plan is to lead the public with new products rather than ask them what kind of products they want. The public does not know what is possible, but we do."[11]

You are the expert, and if you can free yourself from the constraints of your historical model, you can begin to expand and reinvent it so that what you sell is more closely aligned with what customers need. That way, when you win, so do they.

Back to construction. DIRTT is a prefabrication company that recognized the inherent flaws of the traditional construction model. Using a four-step process (Plan, Design, Build, Live), the DIRTT approach focuses on providing value at the outsides of the industry's smiling curve rather than at the traditional center.[12] "Plan" and "Design" are two separate, intentional steps through which consultants carefully work to understand the needs of the project and prepare accordingly. "Live" makes sure that the end product is flexible, so that it remains relevant and useful long after the "Build" phase is complete. By looking at a broader spectrum of client needs, empathizing with the end user, and working outside the constraints of the typical construction process, DIRTT has found opportunities to connect with its customer (and generate revenue) that a traditional general contractor never would.

The approach has been wildly successful. DIRTT generates a quarter billion in annual sales, has clocked annualized growth approaching 50 percent, and has been heralded as one of the "rock stars of the new economy."[13] Even more impressive, it has done so in an industry that has seen less-than-stellar growth in North America since the Great Recession.[14] DIRTT isn't just growing, it's blowing the doors off of its traditional peers by responding to consumer needs they're either unaware of or ignoring.

An old-school general contractor considers "Plan" and "Design" the realm of architects and engineers, and "Live" the problem of the owner. But by focusing on "Build"—the low-value middle of the curve—he's ignoring opportunities. And worse, he might be irrelevant in another decade. DIRTT is making millions by thinking more broadly.

Like Apple, Acer, and DIRTT, the opportunity lies in recognizing what the family really *needs*—and then obsessively building your company around the singular purpose of meeting them there. Not only is that the only way to make money in business, it's the only way to help families truly do death right.

Chapter 11
Optimizing to Death

"It is now known that a perfection of planned layout is achieved only by institutions on the point of collapse... During a period of exciting discovery or progress there is no time to plan the perfect headquarters. The time for that comes later, when all the important work has been done. Perfection, we know, is finality; and finality is death."[1]

Cyril Northcote Parkinson was a British naval historian who coined a number of iterations of "Parkinson's Law," which deals with administration and management. Perhaps most interesting is "Parkinson's Law of Buildings," stated above.[2] He observed a number of cases to prove his point that planned headquarters are evidence of the irrelevance of the organization constructing them.

According to Parkinson, the Vatican was built only after the Papacy had declined in geopolitical influence. The Palace of Nations, the headquarters of the League of Nations, was opened in 1937, four years after the League was declared a failure. Louis XIV's power weakened after his move into Versailles. And King George V laid the cornerstone of New Delhi, founded by the British as a seat of colonial power, in 1911, roughly five years into the decline of British imperialism.[3]

The law works as well metaphorically as it does literally. The "time to plan the perfect headquarters" comes only when "all the important work has been done," but the same could be said of the perfect sales process, the perfect GPL, or the perfect business model. To *innovate* is evidence of the pursuit of the customer. But you can *optimize* while forgetting the customer altogether.

This is an important, and sobering, reminder for the modern funeral home. In no other industry have I observed such a staunch devotion to optimization. In the states where such lists are available, funeral home owners will meticulously count their case numbers against their competitors. Contract averages (by location, by funeral director, and by product type) are scrutinized closely. National consultancies command hefty fees by aggregating and licensing data so that you know how your funeral home measures up against your peers on any of hundreds of data points and variables. Outside of Major League Baseball, nobody knows stats like a mortuary owner.

There's nothing wrong, necessarily, with optimizing. Data, standards, metrics, and benchmarks can all be helpful in exposing blind spots in your tactical approach to business. But one must never miss the forest for the trees. The myriad data points you track in a given month make sense only insofar as they relate to a fixed model. The further afield you move from the tried, the true, the standard, and the expected—the more you innovate—the more difficult it will be to find data points against which to optimize.

Historical data provides clarity, but not completeness. If you're staring at spreadsheets looking for the next opportunity, you're doing it wrong. The poet John Milton wrote about a boat that anchors itself to a sea monster, mistaking its giant back for an island.[4] It's a powerful analogy because the ship would have been safer out at sea where things seemed much more dangerous. False security is a far more lethal threat than recognized uncertainty. Optimizing your business compared to a vast network of your peers feels safe because familiarity feels safe. A graph showing a clear trend, or a strategy built on your old strongholds, is appealing. But it might be fatal if the entire industry is about to take a dive, with you anchored to its back.

You only count the number of bodies you get each month if you've really bought into the notion that you'll always have the body. Otherwise, you'd be keeping a different score because you'd be playing a different game. Moreover, those figures are only helpful if the model they reflect is correct. If bodies aren't the core of your business, they're the wrong thing to count.

You only count the total number of families served if you really believe in being all things to all people. Otherwise, serving fewer families in a month wouldn't be a mark of failure—it would be an indicator that you're working with greater clarity and specificity.

And total revenue is only *the* metric if you're indifferent as to *how* you're making money. If you were focused on aligning incentives with families, you would be looking to optimize revenue per family, or better still, to grow specific types of price structures built for different families' needs. Kodak's total revenue was sky-high at the moment it decided to bury the digital camera.[5, 6] So was Blockbuster's when it laughed Netflix out of the room.[7, 8]

When you're looking at your data in Column A and your peers' data in Column B and the industry standards in Column C, you're not looking at all at the family sitting in your foyer. They don't have a column. They might have needs that your peers have never thought of. They might have a history or an expectation that can't be captured on a spreadsheet. All the important work you're doing to optimize your business against industry standards might very well be the work of erecting a perfectly laid-out headquarters as you're becoming obsolete.

That's why baseball can afford to obsess over stats. The rules of the game are fixed. The league might change a rule here or there once in a while, but there's a high degree of confidence that next season is going to have the same overall format as last season. Within that sort of a closed system, you can afford to optimize. But outside of it, you can never stop thinking about how the game is going to change, even while you simultaneously strengthen your own bench. There's a lot more up in the air in business than in baseball.

In business, momentum beats perfection. You can drive, or you can tinker all day with the engine. There is a time for both, but if you spend all your time under the hood, you're not going to go anywhere. And certainly not anywhere new.

The reason Parkinson's Law of Buildings is true is that focusing on constructing the perfect headquarters, or on optimizing generally, necessarily takes the focus off of the primary work. We remember fondly the days when a now-famous startup (or legendary band) worked out of a garage. Rarely is the group able to recapture the spontaneous creativity and inventiveness of that period, even when it moves into custom-built settings. Whether it's occupied by the Ramones or Bill Gates, the garage yields art in its purest form, unpolluted by distraction. Once you get a taste of success, you become preoccupied with keeping it—which can paradoxically detract from the work that made you relevant and successful in the first place.

The founder of your mortuary, whether it was fifty or one hundred and fifty years ago, didn't have a notion of "always having the body." He simply saw a need, and he filled it. At the turn of the last century, people needed help delivering on the exacting societal and social expectations around death. To prepare a body, (literally) dig a grave, host the necessary events and ceremonies, and provide for all necessary catering, notices, and communication was a daunting task, and one that didn't leave much room for the grieving process. Today few of those societal pressures still exist, and a mortuary inflicts burdens as often as it alleviates them. Optimization, then, may be a distraction from the real work of invention that needs to be done. If the car is traveling in the wrong direction, making it go faster is not helpful.

Nor was the local undertaker all things to all people. In fact, he was likely very few things at all. He didn't have a retort. There was no extensive list of casket options. He had one horse-drawn hearse. His was primarily a service business, existing to help organize a procession, plan a wake, or dig a grave. And the traditions by which he did so were likely limited to a short list of practices and rituals familiar to him. That's precisely what gave him his credibility. You went to church with him, or you were a member of the same fraternal organization. And if you weren't, you might go to his competitor instead.

And he probably wasn't as worried as you are about tracking month-to-month merchandise sales. He didn't have a GPL or, if he did, it was a tenth the length of yours. And he made no apologies for it. Optimization in sales, like optimization in other categories, assumes a fixed playbook. If you're staring at month-over-month figures and wondering how to boost casket averages, jewelry averages, and urn averages all at the same time, your problem might not be your averages. It might be the assumption that you can excel at everything. Instead of optimizing, maybe you need to decide what it is you want to be great at.

Optimization in sales, too, obscures the challenges of today in the long shadow of the industry's heyday. Your grandfather didn't have much merchandise to sell—he certainly wasn't worried about how to sell more of it per case. Instead, he was innovating and changing based on families' interests. A motorized hearse here; in-home funeral preparations there. If you're trying to figure out how to sell *more* of the same thing month over month, you've already skipped past (or anchored yourself to) a more important decision about *what* to sell in the first place. And that shouldn't be a one-time decision.

Success means taking your eyes off your spreadsheets and fixing them obsessively on families. What do they want? What might be bothering them? What would make their lives easier? These questions cannot be answered by optimization, because optimization is based on a fixed presumption: keep doing what you're doing, only better. But what families need from you might be something altogether different. And meeting that need might mean abandoning old approaches and assumptions, rather than honing them.

If changing bad industry habits all at once feels daunting, fear not. "We'll always have the body," "We must be all things to all people," and "Merchandise matters" are not themselves decision points. They are broad, foundational assumptions. Moving away from those assumptions does require decision, but in execution it's done through tiny, bite-sized moves. You don't have to rebuild your entire business at once. Deciding to change how to sell, how to work, or how to make money is not a switch you can flip as the result of a single strategic planning session. It's a change in mindset that will redefine how you think for the remainder of your career.

As you set out to transform your mortuary (assuming that's what you want to do), perhaps the best way to think of the Three Lies is as a series of filters. With every independent business decision, be it a hire, a new product, a price, a remodel, or any other type of investment, having awareness of the faulty assumptions in your business will help you begin to transcend them. It would be impossible to completely rid your firm this week of the assumption that you will always have the body. But you can, over the course of years, evaluate every choice you make within the context of that awareness: "Will this hire make us more complacent, or less?" "Will this move keep us dependent on disposition, or help us move to higher ground?" "Am I thinking this way because I'm assuming we'll always have the body?"

Every decision you make is made through the filters of your own biases and assumptions. Some of these are conscious, some are subconscious, and some are entirely unconscious (simply "in the water" of funeral service). Through the practical, day-to-day management of your firm, an intentional choice to add new filters will invariably help you move in a healthy direction.

As you begin to do so, some decisions will be of more pressing importance than others. The Three Lies (and the corresponding adjustments to your business model that overcoming them will require) have big, long-term ramifications that you won't be able to turn on a dime. But they do have some immediate implications for your firm. And if you want to start addressing them, there are some immediate, practical steps that must be taken to put you on a path back toward growth.

Choose a path.

Before you can change anything, you have to decide what you're changing for. Do you believe in guiding families toward a "right way," or are you willing to provide whatever they ask for? Is your work a ministry first and foremost, or just a way to make a living? What (and how) are you willing to sell? What are you not willing to sell? Does the thought of being acquired by a conglomerate make you sick, or do you consider it a valid endgame that could let you get out at the right time? Is your objective to keep the firm in the family for another hundred years? Or just to make it to retirement?

If your reading of the tea leaves leads you to believe that you can succeed by doing things the way you always have, then that's an answer in itself. But if it doesn't, you must start with a hard look in the mirror and some intentional decisions about what you're aiming for—and why. A change in destination will affect every other decision a pilot makes. You must set an objective above all. You don't have to do it alone, but you do have to choose a single path.

Deal with succession.

Discussions about change and reinvention might be moot if the driver isn't in the driver's seat. Whether you're the incoming leader or the outgoing one, odds are there are succession decisions in your firm that need to be dealt with. If that's not the case, seize the moment. You're in a rare position that should be exploited; most of your peers envy your autonomy and the agility that comes with it.

If pending succession issues are impacting your firm, start dealing with them. Your staff may not be wringing their hands over who takes over next, but the benefit to morale and internal clarity of having those decisions wrapped up is immense. People appreciate that you're intentionally making decisions to keep their futures secure. And you can only help families deal with the speck in their eyes if you've first pulled the plank out of yours. Looming succession can be an immense burden and distraction. Get it dealt with.

Face your blind spots.

This can be the hardest piece to do alone. Do you have a mentor or confidant who understands your business and is able to point out weaknesses? Who would know if you've become complacent in your business model, or desperate in your sales processes, or if you are sacrificing trust for revenue? Healthy athletes require coaches, healthy churches require pastors, and healthy businesses require accountability. It's all but impossible to do surgery on yourself. Success in the fairest of circumstances requires an honest perspective, far enough removed to give you painful truth and to prescribe medicine you don't want to take. Amidst stale and commoditized business conditions, you cannot afford to go it alone.

There are many options for where to find good mentorship and accountability, but that doesn't mean they're all equally valid. The right accountability partners must be able to be completely honest with you. Family members or business partners don't count. These people might be able to provide some good advice, but their proximity to you or their vested interests in the status quo might make them stay silent when they need to speak up.

An accountability partner should also have enough familiarity with your business to knowledgeably discuss it, but not enough that they share the same prejudices and assumptions that you bring to the table. This is perhaps the toughest criterion to meet. Most people will either fall too close or too far away. Rotary clubs or Vistage groups can offer outstanding opportunities to swap insights and gain outside perspective, but often your peers in those circles will lack the experience in funeral service to speak to your model and decisions with any helpful specificity. Conversely, trade associations are so heavily steeped in the status quo (and incentivized to protect it) that they can be great for optimization, but rarely yield meaningful innovation. That's one of the reasons real innovation within established industries is so rare, and it's why finding the right training partner is so important if you want to break through.

Go on the offensive.

Most private American funeral homes are family-owned—some in their fourth or fifth generation. The benefits of this in terms of family pride, heritage, and legacy are immense. To train for business your whole life has considerable advantages over coming into it in your twenties or thirties.

One disadvantage of this model, however, is the fact that it often breeds a mindset of playing *not to lose* rather than playing to win. A brash young captain of a new warship is going to take substantially greater risks than the captain of a delicate antique vessel that his grandfather piloted.

Entrepreneurs are inherently aggressive and comfortable with risk; they don't want to go out of business, but they also want to make a return on their investment. But the pressure of sharing Thanksgiving dinner with the two or three people who ran the company before you took over can be utterly debilitating. It can feel like the only goal is keep it afloat for a few more years—to not be the one on whose watch the lights went out. In the face of that pressure "not to lose," playing to actually win—to innovate, to take calculated risks, and to seek out new sources of momentum—often gets forgotten.

But the best defense is a good offense. Brands that hunker down and try to wait out the storm are never industry leaders. Navel-gazing is a symptom of dying brands—a truth confirmed by decades of business research by my firm.

Your marketing. Your business model. Your GPL. Your hiring strategy. Your overhead structure. Your portfolio of brands. Your training model. Your website. In every one of these is a detail that you inherited, whether from a previous generation or from an industry norm. Perhaps you can sense it is just a bit off. Fix it. Make a change. Make an investment. Get on the move. Take the risk. If you don't, you'll never score a point, let alone win a game.

Get serious online.

Your website might be just the place to start going on the offensive. You'll spend a million dollars on a new location and call it an "investment," but families will make a decision about your firm based on your website long before they walk in your doors—or even give you a call. And they're more likely to Google "funeral home near me" than they are to drive past your fancy new branch.

You get what you pay for. Funeral homes are plagued by the notion that websites should be free. But what kind of office would you expect if you build your next building with a general contractor who worked for a percentage of flower sales? If you don't have a strategy in place to aggressively and consistently improve your site, differentiate your brand online, and win in Google rankings, you are playing to lose.

That means scrutinizing your site through the eyes of a grieving family to make sure that nothing seems untoward or ill-considered. It means having a solid, ongoing plan for site maintenance and fine-tuning for search engine optimization (SEO) on a regular basis. It means investing in new plugins and technologies to make online planning easier (or possible) for families. It means dedicated monthly SEO, paid search, and retargeting budgets, at a minimum. And it means investing in a website provider who is going to challenge you and fight for your turf—not sell a duplicate site to a competitor.

Most of all, it means never saying you're "done" with your website. Your firm's digital presence *is* its presence. It merits every bit the investment, and should be taken every bit as seriously, as your physical locations.

Take small risks.

Before Scatter Day took root as an international phenomenon, we spent years trying out a handful of other (more expensive) concepts toward the same end. Willingness to try new things, and to do so continually, is vital to the success of any business. In Chapter 8 we discussed the importance of taking small risks and the idea of establishing an annual innovation budget. Amazon sold windshield wipers as a first step toward selling everything (instead of just books).[9] Online streaming was initially a side project for Netflix.[10] Lego made one of the most famous turnarounds in business history by introducing a small-risk policy by which the company would prototype inventive toys and double down on the experiments that worked. The approach led to the end of hundreds of failed product lines—and the creation of some of its all-time best sellers.[11]

If you don't have the willingness to make small moves and take small risks, it's unlikely you will ever be able to make the big moves by which an old, established brand can earn big returns.

Start.

Momentum beats perfection. Pick something on this list and get to work on it. But make this promise to yourself: if in a month you haven't made any headway on any of the above six items, get help. We all hire outside experts for accountability in all sorts of areas, from personal trainers to doctors to financial planners to... funeral directors. There's no shame in seeking outside expertise to address the challenges and stagnancy in your own business. Just as you tell families about the benefits of pre-planning, if you've been putting it off, there's no better time than the present to take action.

Somewhere out there is a family about to experience a loss. That reality has motivated you for years—perhaps for your entire life. They're going to be feeling about their grief everything you're feeling right now about your company: paralyzed by all the work to be done, confused by what to do first, and unsure of their ability to get through it. They don't need a newfangled entrepreneur who understands the internet more than he understands human hearts. They don't need a waiter, notepad in hand, to ask what they want, because they probably don't even know. And they don't need more doubt, more confusion, and more uncertainty—they have all that in spades.

What they need is someone called to lead them. Someone with the gift of guiding, gently and with their best interests at heart. Someone with the ability to shepherd and protect and serve them through what may well be the very worst day of their lives. In the midst of that pain, and weight, and numbing shock, they need someone to provide some semblance of hope. Comfort. Clarity. Few know how to offer these to a grieving family. Fewer can lead a business that delivers them. And even fewer can do so *right*—with the right heart, the right approach, and for the right reasons.

But you can. It's time to answer the call.

Epilogue

Dear Ms. Mitford,

Please forgive the tardiness of this reply. Your public criticism of "the funeral men" was owed a response much sooner. Fifty-seven years is a long time to wait for an answer.

Thank you for bringing to our attention your very serious concerns. When you caught our industry admitting that the sale of certain products and services is more in the funeral director's interest than the family's, you were right. We're sorry for that legacy, and we've spent the decades since working hard to remedy it. And when you caught a few of us encouraging families to overspend on funerals to atone for neglecting their loved ones, you were right again. It's safe to say there are few in funeral service today who would espouse such a view—something of which both you, and we who believe in our calling, can be proud.

Our complaint with your work, after six decades of reflection, is that you didn't go far enough. After all, if the grievances you so angrily leveled against us were true, the remedies you suggested were rather pitiful. You seemed more worried about the problems than the solutions, and as a result, we still don't have many solutions.

You called our work "patently fraudulent," and said we make a habit of "preying on the grief, remorse, and guilt of survivors." You took pains to clarify that these attacks were leveled at "the vast majority" of our profession, whom you claim devised and manipulated codes of conduct "for [our] own purposes." You said we've propped up the whole charade with "a new mythology," and have "invented" terminology, traditions, and even diagnoses for the purpose of conning the public.

If funeral service is really such a vast and deeply rooted conspiracy, then surely you knew that a handful of feeble workarounds would hardly be able to make a dent. Nor could you have seriously believed that the Funeral Rule, in support of which you so gleefully testified, would solve the problem. After all, it's hard to think of a federally regulated industry that hasn't still managed to create rather disastrous situations for its customers.

Really, we wish you would have helped funeral directors understand the pain that results when we neglect our duty to lead and guide families. You recognized even better than we did that our calling suffers from a split personality, but rather than helping to heal that split, you widened it.

Today, families still need the guidance we can provide, but the seeds of doubt you sowed have grown into a hedgerow that separates us from them. Since you arbitrarily decided that only psychologists can wade into the waters of grief, you cut us off as a source of experienced support. And, as numerous psychologists have written, a chance to come together and mourn the deceased is vital for healthy communities. But you preached that the funeral is a "grotesque cloud-cuckoo-land," and a "full-fledged burlesque," "methodically designed and tailored to extract maximum profit." You did a great job of convincing people to avoid us. But you threw out the baby with the bathwater, leaving the bereaved without the communal farewell they still (and always will) need.

It's clear that you did all of this to spite "the funeral men." What's less clear is that anybody has been able to mourn better or more healthfully since you liberated the world from us.

A fifth of Americans today have cremated remains at home—many of those sheepishly stashed away in closets and basements. Was that the legacy you wanted? Fewer people are embalmed today, but much of that revenue has shifted to the sale of mass-produced trinkets—we're not sure you'd see that as an improvement. And many of the funeral men you so despised have gone out of business, but a newer, stranger kind of enterprise has taken their place, productizing the human body in everything from jewelry to shotgun shells to space dust. There is a new American way of death, but it's hard to see how it's any better than the one you condemned.

We really wish you'd aimed at the heart of the problem. Embalming was an obsession of yours, but time has shown that it was just a lurid distraction from the real issues at hand. After all, it was the prettying up and sanitization of death that you so reviled—"decorating [the deceased] with paint and powder"—but your heirs have, under your influence, used direct cremation to only further sanitize and distance themselves from the realities of death. If observing a preserved corpse is an exercise in self-deception, how much more so are cremated remains sitting on mantelpieces and referred to by name as if "she's still here?" A cloisonné whitewashing is hardly better than a formaldehyde one.

You were spot-on about many things. People were spending a lot of money on funerals, and funeral directors were making a lot of money because of it. Some unethically so. By and large, that has changed. But many things haven't. People still die. Death is still disorienting. The bereaved still need help. The body must still be laid to rest. Religious and cultural traditions still provide healing and solace. Amidst all of these needs, you gave the public plenty to doubt, but nothing and nobody to trust.

We must do better. We hope we have. And we know there is still a great deal of work to be done. But for nearly all its history, humanity (not to mention a good part of the animal kingdom) has processed grief actively, deliberately, and communally. Whether intentionally or not, your work has helped to make grief cheap, unceremonious, and isolated.

We wish that, instead of going to such extremes to put us out of business, you would have helped us do our business better. You were correct that the bereaved must never be only a means to profit. But you were wrong that a lifetime of service to the dead and mourning can be caustically dismissed as "a huge, macabre, and expensive practical joke."

Better days are ahead. We will redouble our efforts to serve families with dignity, to honor the memories of the deceased, and to earn the trust of our communities. Our hope is that we may someday help members of your family to mourn their own relatives. To do so has always been, and will remain, our highest honor.

Sincerely,

The Funeral Men (and Women)

Notes

Introduction

1   Jessica Mitford, *The American Way of Death Revisited* (New York: Knopf Doubleday Publishing Group, 2011), 13.

Chapter 1

1   Caitlin Doughty, *Smoke Gets in Your Eyes: And Other Lessons from the Crematory* (New York: W. W. Norton & Company, 2014), 107.

2   Funeral Consumers Alliance, "Inaugural Issue," *The Grim Reader*, Fall 2012, 1, https://funerals.org/wp-content/uploads/2016/06/grim-reader-fall-2012.pdf

3   Jessica Mitford, *The American Way of Death Revisited* (New York: Knopf Doubleday Publishing Group, 2011), 12-13.

4   Mitford, 13.

5   Mitford, 13.

6   Judith Newman, "Books in Brief: Nonfiction." *The New York Times.* October 4, 1998. https://www.nytimes.com/1998/10/04/books/books-in-brief-nonfiction-026573.html

7   Patrick Vlaskovits, "Henry Ford, Innovation, and That 'Faster Horse' Quote," Harvard Business Review, Aug. 29, 2011, https://hbr.org/2011/08/henry-ford-never-said-the-fast.

8   Barbara Farfan, "What is Apple's Mission Statement?," *the balance everyday*, November 20, 2019, https://www.thebalanceeveryday.com/apple-mission-statement-4068547.

9   McKee Wallwork + Co., *The Death Care Disruption Index*, report produced in collaboration with Selected Independent Funeral Homes, Sept. 2019, 42.

10   McKee Wallwork + Co., *Death Care Disruption Index*, 36.

11   McKee Wallwork + Co., *Death Care Disruption Index*, 14.

12   Tom Nichols, *The Death of Expertise: The Campaign Against Established Knowledge and Why It Matters* (New York: Oxford University Press, 2017), 1.

13   Nichols, 83.

Chapter 2

1   Rachel Nuwer, "This Japanese Shrine Has Been Torn Down And Rebuilt Every 20 Years for the Past Millenium," *Smithsonian Magazine: SmartNews*, October 4, 2014, https://www.smithsonianmag.com/smart-news/this-japanese-shrine-has-been-torn-down-and-rebuilt-every-20-years-for-the-past-millennium-575558/.

2   Austin Brown, "Alexander Rose Visits Ise Shrine Reconstruction Ceremony," *The Long Now Foundation*, October 3, 2013, https://blog.longnow.org/02013/10/03/alexander-rose-visits-ise-shrine-reconstruction-ceremony/.

3   Institute of Medicine (U.S.) Committee on Care at the End of Life, *Approaching Death: Improving Care at the End of Life*, ed. Marilyn J. Field and Christine K. Cassel (Washington, D.C: National Academies Press, 1997), 33.

4   Institute of Medicine (U.S.) Committee on Care at the End of Life, 33.

5   Life expectancy at birth for the average American was only slightly over 50 years in 1920. It rose rapidly between then and the mid-1950s, when figures began to exceed 70 years. Institute of Medicine (U.S.) Committee on Care at the End of Life, 33. See also Centers for Disease Control and Prevention, *Life expectancy at birth, at age 65, and at age 75, by sex, race, and Hispanic origin: United States, selected years 1900–2017*, 2018, last reviewed October 30, 2019, https://www.cdc.gov/nchs/data/hus/2018/004.pdf.

6   The Wharton School of the University of Pennsylvania, "Mortality in the United States: Past, Present, and Future," *Budget Model*, June 27, 2016, https://budgetmodel.wharton.upenn.edu/issues/2016/1/25/mortality-in-the-united-states-past-present-and-future.

7   Institute of Medicine (U.S.) Committee on Care at the End of Life, *Approaching Death*, 33.

8   Kimberly Leonard, "America's Health Care Elixir," *US News*, July 30, 2015, https://www.usnews.com/news/the-report/articles/2015/07/30/medicare-changed-health-care-in-america-for-the-better.

9   Jason Rodriquez, *Labors of Love: Nursing Homes and the Structures of Care Work* (New York: New York University Press, 2014), 172.

10   William H. Thomas, *What Are Old People For?: How Elders Will Save the World* (St. Louis MO: VanderWyk & Burnham, 2004), 77.

11   *Living Arrangements of the Elderly* (U.S. Department of Commerce, Economics and Statistics Administration, Bureau of the Census, 1993), 3:4.

12   Brian Walsh, "When You Die, You'll Probably Be Embalmed. Thank Abraham Lincoln For That," *Smithsonian Magazine*, November 1, 2017, https://www.smithsonianmag.com/science-nature/how-lincolns-embrace-embalming-birthed-american-funeral-industry-180967038/.

13 Samantha Watson, *A History of Funerals in the United States*, July 12, 2016, https://www.frazerconsultants.com/2016/07/a-history-of-funerals-in-the-united-states/.

14 Maggie Jones, "The Movement to Bring Death Closer," *The New York Times Magazine*, December 19, 2019, updated January 13, 2020, https://www.nytimes.com/2019/12/19/magazine/home-funeral.html.

15 WKYT News Staff, "Family digs woman's grave after burial plot left unfinished before funeral," *WKYT*, December 8, 2017, https://www.wkyt.com/content/news/Family-digs-womans-grave-after-burial-plot-left-unfinished-before-funeral-462867933.html.

16 16 Pew Research Center, *America's Changing Religious Landscape*, May 12, 2015, https://www.pewforum.org/2015/05/12/americas-changing-religious-landscape/.

17 Jay L. Zagorsky, "Why are fewer people getting married?" *The Conversation,* June 1, 2016, https://theconversation.com/why-are-fewer-people-getting-married-60301.

18 Sharon Johnson, "No-Fault Divorce: 10 Years Later, Some Virtues, Some Flaws," *New York Times*, March 30, 1979, 22, https://www.nytimes.com/1979/03/30/archives/nofault-divorce-10-years-later-some-virtues-some-flaws-only-three.html.

19 Mary Fetzer, "By the numbers: A breakdown of divorce by generation," AvvoStories, April 12, 2017, https://stories.avvo.com/relationships/divorce/numbers-breakdown-divorce-generation.html.

20 Harvard School of Public Health—MetLife Foundation Initiative on Retirement and Civic Engagement, *Reinventing Aging: Baby Boomers and Civic Engagement* (Boston: Center for Health Communication Harvard School of Public Health, 2004), https://assets.aarp.org/rgcenter/general/boomers_engagement.pdf.

21 Lyman Stone, "The Boomers Ruined Everything: The mistakes of the past are fast creating a crisis for younger Americans," *The Atlantic*, June 24, 2019, https://www.theatlantic.com/ideas/archive/2019/06/boomers-are-blame-aging-america/592336/.

22 Stone, https://www.theatlantic.com/ideas/archive/2019/06/boomers-are-blame-aging-america/592336/.

23 Stone, https://www.theatlantic.com/ideas/archive/2019/06/boomers-are-blame-aging-america/592336/.

24 Peter F. Drucker, *The Age of Discontinuity: Guidelines to Our Changing Society* (Amsterdam, Netherlands: Elsevier Publishing Company, 2013), 290.

25 Google Trends, "What to do when someone dies," accessed August 9, 2020, https://trends.google.com/trends/explore?q=%22what%20to%20do%20when%20someone%20dies%22.

26 Google Trends, "How much does cremation cost," accessed August 9, 2020, https://trends.google.com/trends/explore?q=%22how%20much%20does%20cremation%20cost%22.

27 Google Trends, "Celebration of Life," accessed August 9, 2020, https://trends.google.com/trends/explore?q=%22Celebration%20of%20Life%22.

28 Google Trends, "Grief Resources," accessed August 9, 2020, https://trends.google.com/trends/explore?q=%22Grief%20Resources%22.

Chapter 3

1   Winston S. Churchill, *The Story of the Malakand Field Force* (London, 1898; repr. Whitefish, MT: Kessinger Publishing, 2004), 170.

2   Doug Zanger, "These Former Nike Executives Are Looking to Disrupt the Death Care Industry," *AdWeek*, April 11, 2019, https://www.adweek.com/brand-marketing/these-former-nike-executives-are-looking-to-disrupt-the-death-care-industry/.

3   Danny Fortson, "Tulip: Silicon Valley's no-frills journey to cremation," *The Times,* January 12, 2020, https://www.thetimes.co.uk/edition/business/tulip-silicon-valleys-no-frills-journey-to-cremation-mf6lrn58p.

4   Erin Chambers, "Costco: Coffins in Aisle 9," *Bloomberg News*, August 17, 2004, https://www.bloomberg.com/news/articles/2004-08-17/costco-coffins-in-aisle-9.

5   Lib Copel, "A Dead Ringer for The Dearly Departed," *Wall Street Journal,* December 30, 2002, https://www.washingtonpost.com/archive/lifestyle/2002/12/30/a-dead-ringer-for-the-dearly-departed/408ce9b2-e723-4956-a3f7-d774f4080207/.

6   These include the International End of Life Doula Association (INELDA), https://www.inelda.org/, and the National End-of-Life Doula Alliance (NEDA), http://www.doulaprogram.org/.

7   Empowered Widow, accessed June 19, 2020, http://www.empoweredwidow.com/; Going in Style, accessed June 19, 2020, https://www.funeral-consulting.com/.

8   Everest Funeral Concierge, accessed June 19, 2020, https://everestfuneral.com/.

9   Funeralocity, accessed June 19, 2020, https://www.funeralocity.com/.

10 FuneralDecisions.com, accessed June 19, 2020, https://www.funeraldecisions.com/; Final Moments Concierge Services, accessed June 19, 2020, https://finalmomentsconcierge.com/; Funerals360, accessed June 19, 2020, https://www.funerals360.com/.

11 SimpleCremationOnline, accessed June 19, 2020, https://www.simplecremationonline.com/; BasicFunerals and Cremation Choices, accessed June 19, 2020, https://basicfunerals.ca/.

12 Cake, https://www.joincake.com/account/onboarding/; GYST, https://getyourshittogether.org/; Everplans, https://www.everplans.com/; AfterNote, https://www.afternote.com/; FuneralWise, https://www.funeralwise.com/; Beyond, https://beyond.life/; DyingMatters.org, https://www.dyingmatters.org/; Digital Legacy Association, https://digitallegacyassociation.org/; Ghost Memo, https://www.ghostmemo.com/; LifeNaut, https://www.lifenaut.com/. All websites above accessed on June 19, 2020.

13 LifeNaut.com, accessed June 19, 2020, https://www.lifenaut.com/.

14 The Natural Death Centre, accessed June 19, 2020, http://www.naturaldeath.org.uk/; Green Burial Council, accessed June 19, 2020, https://www.greenburialcouncil.org/.

15 Natural Burial Company, accessed June 19, 2020, https://www.naturalburialcompany.com/; Passages International, accessed June 19, 2020, https://www.passagesinternational.com/; Ecopods, accessed June 19, 2020, https://www.ecopod.co.uk/.

16   Coeio.com, accessed June 19, 2020, https://coeio.com/.

17   Capsula Mundi, accessed June 19, 2020, https://www.capsulamundi.it/en/.

18   The Living Urn, accessed August 7, 2020, https://www.thelivingurn.com/pages/tree-zip-code.

19   Eternal Reefs, accessed June 19, 2020, https://www.eternalreefs.com/.

20   Recompose, accessed June 19, 2020, https://www.recompose.life/faq.

21   Ed Defort, "19 States Now Permit Alkaline Hydrolysis," *Memorial Business Journal*, June 13, 2019, posted by the Arizona Funeral, Cemetery, and Crematory Association, https://azfcca.org/19-states-now-permit-alkaline-hydrolysis/.

22   Cremains At Sea, accessed June 19, 2020, https://www.cremainsatsea.com/details.php.

23   Eternal Ascent Society, accessed June 19, 2020, https://sites.google.com/view/etern alascenthome?pli=1&authuser=3/; A Journey With Wings, accessed June 19, 2020, https://www.ajourneywithwings.com/.

24   Elysium Space, accessed June 19, 2020, https://elysiumspace.com/; Celestis, accessed June 19, 2020, https://www.celestis.com/experiences-pricing/.

25   Heavens Above Fireworks, accessed June 19, 2020, https://www.heavensabovefire-works.com/.

26   My Holy Smoke, accessed June 19, 2020, http://www.myholysmoke.com/.

27   Cremation Solutions, accessed June 19, 2020, https://www.cremationsolutions.com/the-loved-one-launcher-ash-scattering-cannon.

28   Bernhard Schroeder, "Baby Boomers Are Fueling an Industry That Is Ripe For Disruption. The Rise of The Death Concierge," *Forbes*, April 15, 2019, https://www.forbes.com/sites/bernhardschroeder/2019/04/15/baby-boomers-are-fueling-an-industry-that-is-ripe-for-disruption-the-rise-of-the-death-concierge.

29   Allie Volpe, "Disruption comes for death: Cremation is on the rise. Whimsical and environmentally friendly businesses are changing the final frontier," *Vox*, May 23, 2019, https://www.vox.com/the-goods/2019/5/23/18635971/cremation-sustainable-funeral-eco-friendly-alternatives-burial.

30   Maggie Jones, "The Movement to Bring Death Closer," *The New York Times Magazine*, December 19, 2020, updated January 13, 2020, https://www.nytimes.com/2019/12/19/magazine/home-funeral.html.

31   *Lexico*, s.v. "Disruption," Oxford University Press, accessed June 19, 2020, https://www.lexico.com/definition/disruption.

32   McKee Wallwork + Co., *The Death Care Disruption Index*, report produced in collaboration with Selected Independent Funeral Homes, Sept. 2019, 10.

33   McKee Wallwork + Co., *Death Care Disruption Index*, 11.

34   McKee Wallwork + Co., *Death Care Disruption Index*, 16.

35 McKee Wallwork + Co., *Death Care Consumer Segmentation Study*, unpublished report, August 2011, Microsoft PowerPoint file.

36 McKee Wallwork + Co., *Death Care Consumer Segmentation Study*, unpublished report, August 2011, Microsoft PowerPoint file.

37 McKee Wallwork + Co., *Death Care Preferences Survey*, unpublished report, Mar. 10, 2020, Microsoft PowerPoint file.

38 McKee Wallwork + Co., *Death Care Preferences Survey*, 2020.

39 McKee Wallwork + Co., *Death Care Consumer Segmentation Study*, 2011.

40 Brad Stone, "Uber: the app that changed how the world hails a taxi," *The Guardian*, January 29, 2017, https://www.theguardian.com/technology/2017/jan/29/uber-app-changed-how-world-hails-a-taxi-brad-stone.

Chapter 4

1 Jessica Mitford, *The American Way of Death Revisited* (New York: Knopf Doubleday Publishing Group, 2011), 64.

2 Mitford, 64.

3 Mitford, 66.

4 Mitford, 65.

5 Mitford, 64.

6 Mitford, 64

7 Mitford, 65

8 Mitford, 65.

9 J. William Worden, *Grief Counseling and Grief Therapy: A Handbook for the Mental Health Practitioner*, 3rd ed. (New York: Springer Publishing, 2002).

10 Dan Bates, "The 4 Tasks of Grieving: Grieving is a healthy response to loss," *Psychology Today*, November 8, 2019, https://www.psychologytoday.com/us/blog/mental-health-nerd/201911/the-4-tasks-grieving.

11 Worden, *Grief Counseling*, see esp. 27-37.

12 Dorian & Daniel, dirs., "Dear Brother," Johnnie Walker, posted December 14, 2015, https://www.youtube.com/watch?v=h2caT4q4Nbs.

13 Worden, *Grief Counseling*, 27.

14 "New Study Shows Americans Recognize the Role of Memorialization in Healthy Healing Following the Death of a Loved One," Funeral and Memorial Information Council, April 2015, accessed July 21, 2020, https://www.famic.org/famic-study/.

15 Skylawn Funeral Home and Memorial Park, "One in Five People Have Cremated Remains at Home," *Businesswire*, December 29, 2014, https://www.businesswire.com/news/home/20141229005026/en/People-Cremated-Remains-Home.

16 Mary Lynn Smith, "Putting off the final farewells: In an increasingly mobile world, more people are delaying family funerals," *StarTribune*, March 7, 2011, https://www.startribune.com/putting-off-the-final-farewells/117558463/.

17 Karl E. Jennings, *When We Must Say Farewell* (Olivet, MI: 2 Moon Press, 2010).

18 "Insights into the Acute Loss Period: What Is the Acute Loss Period?," Borek Jennings Funeral Homes, accessed June 27, 2020, https://www.borekjennings.com/acute-loss-period.

19 Alan D. Wolfelt, *Funeral Home Customer Service A-Z: Creating Exceptional Experiences for Today's Families* (Fort Collins, CO: Companion Center Press, 2004), 212-215.

20 Shifra Goldenberg, "Rare Footage: Wild Elephants 'Mourn' Their Dead," YouTube video, National Geographic YouTube Channel, uploaded September 2, 2016, https://www.youtube.com/watch?v=Ku_GUNzXoeQ.

21 Goldenberg, https://www.youtube.com/watch?v=Ku_GUNzXoeQ.

22 Barry Yeoman, "When Animals Grieve," The National Wildlife Federation, January 3, 2018, https://www.nwf.org/Home/Magazines/National-Wildlife/2018/Feb-Mar/Animals/When-Animals-Grieve.

23 Kelli Bender, "Grieving Dog Attends Owner's Funeral and Finds Peace Again After Pet Parent's Sudden Death," *People*, May 9, 2018, https://people.com/pets/grieving-dog-attends-owners-funeral/.

24 Michael Hanlon, "Is this haunting picture proof that chimps really DO grieve?," *Daily Mail*, October 27, 2009, https://www.dailymail.co.uk/sciencetech/article-1223227/Is-haunting-picture-proof-chimps-really-DO-grieve.html.

25 Alan D. Wolfelt, "Mustering the Courage to Mourn," Center for Loss and Life Transition, December 14, 2016, https://www.centerforloss.com/2016/12/mustering-courage-mourn/.

26 Jennings, *When We Must Say Farewell*, 44.

27 Worden, *Grief Counseling*, 27.

28 Mitford, *American Way of Death Revisited*, 66.

29 Michael I. Norton and Francesca Gino, "Rituals alleviate grieving for loved ones, lovers, and lotteries," *Journal of Experimental Psychology: General* 143, no. 1 (2014): 3, https://pubmed.ncbi.nlm.nih.gov/23398180/.

30 Norton and Gino, 271.

31 Jonathan Jong, "From mummification to 'sky burials': why we need death rituals," *The Conversation*, June 13, 2016, https://theconversation.com/from-mummification-to-sky-burials-why-we-need-death-rituals-60386.

32 Paul C. Rosenblatt, R. Patricia Walsh, and Douglas A. Jackson, *Grief and mourning in cross-cultural perspective*, (New Haven, CT: HRAF Press, 1976), 93.

33 Skylawn Funeral Home and Memorial Park, "One in Five People," https://www.businesswire.com/news/home/20141229005026/en/People-Cremated-Remains-Home.

Chapter 5

1   Jim Collins, *Good to Great: Why Some Companies Make the Leap... and Others Don't* (New York: Random House Business, 2001), 14.

2   Jim Collins, "The Stockdale Paradox," JimCollins.com, accessed July 2, 2020, https://www.jimcollins.com/media_topics/TheStockdaleParadox.html.

3   Jim Collins, "Stockdale Paradox," https://www.jimcollins.com/media_topics/TheStockdaleParadox.html.

4   Marc Randolph, "He 'was struggling not to laugh': Inside Netflix's crazy, doomed meeting with Blockbuster," *Vanity Fair*, September 17, 2019, https://www.vanityfair.com/news/2019/09/netflixs-crazy-doomed-meeting-with-blockbuster.

5   Randolph, https://www.vanityfair.com/news/2019/09/netflixs-crazy-doomed-meeting-with-blockbuster.

6   Claudia H. Deutsch, "At Kodak, Some Old Things Are New Again," *The New York Times*, May 2, 2008, https://www.nytimes.com/2008/05/02/technology/02kodak.html.

7   Giep Franzen and Sandra E. Moriarty, *The Science and Art of Branding* (London: Routledge, 2015), 30.

8   Matthew Fitzgerald, "The iCamera: A look back at Apple's first digital camera," *CNET*, July 28, 2009, https://www.cnet.com/news/the-icamera-a-look-back-at-apples-first-digital-camera/.

9   Haley Morgan, "Proposed Tennessee bill could deregulate licensed professions such as Medical Professionals, Funeral Directors, Engineers, Tattoo Artists, and more," *Coffee County News*, February 14, 2020, http://coffeecountynews.com/proposed-tennessee-bill-could-deregulate-licensed-professions-such-as-medical-professionals-funeral-directors-engineers-tattoo-artists-and-more/.

10 Mike Agogliati, "State will not deregulate funeral homes," *The Register Citizen*, August 5, 2011, https://www.registercitizen.com/news/article/State-will-not-deregulate-funeral-homes-12079184.php.

11 "Wisconsin lawmakers debate deregulation of funeral industry," *TwinCities Pioneer Press*, February 16, 2014, https://www.twincities.com/2014/02/16/wisconsin-lawmakers-debate-deregulation-of-funeral-industry/.

12 T. Scott Gilligan, "Licenses Under Attack," *Memorial Business Journal*, February 27, 2020, https://www.nfda.org/news/in-the-news/nfda-news/id/4912/licenses-under-attack.

13 Gilligan, https://www.nfda.org/news/in-the-news/nfda-news/id/4912/licenses-under-attack.

14 "Monks in Louisiana win lengthy fight to sell caskets," *Catholic News Agency*, October 18, 2013, https://www.catholicnewsagency.com/news/monks-in-louisiana-win-lengthy-fight-to-sell-caskets.

15 For more information on licensing and educational requirements in Colorado, see "Careers in Funeral Service," Colorado Funeral Directors Association, accessed July 7, 2020, https://www.cofda.org/site_page.cfm?pk_association_webpage_menu=7039&pk_association_webpage=14163. Information on laws and regulations in the state may be found at https://www.cofda.org/site_page.cfm?pk_association_webpage_menu=7020&pk_association_webpage=14043.

16 Lindsay Marchello, "Is the funeral business a dying industry?," *Carolina Journal*, October 31, 2017, https://www.carolinajournal.com/news-article/32050/.

17 Anonymous interviewee, Death Care Focus Group 2, McKee Wallwork + Co., April 1, 2019, Albuquerque, NM, Scribie transcript.

18 Sam Gustin, "The Fatal Mistake That Doomed BlackBerry: BlackBerry failed to anticipate that consumers — not business customers — would drive the smartphone revolution," *Time Magazine*, September 24, 2013, https://business.time.com/2013/09/24/the-fatal-mistake-that-doomed-blackberry/.

19 Gustin, https://business.time.com/2013/09/24/the-fatal-mistake-that-doomed-blackberry/.

20 Gustin, https://business.time.com/2013/09/24/the-fatal-mistake-that-doomed-blackberry/.

21 Christopher Helman, "How The Pandemic Is Killing The Death Business," *Forbes*, April 21, 2020, https://www.forbes.com/sites/christopherhelman/2020/04/21/how-the-pandemic-is-killing-the-death-business/#3551d9446c64.

22 Emily Badger, "Taxi medallions have been the best investment in America for years. Now Uber may be changing that," *The Washington Post*, June 20, 2014, https://www.washingtonpost.com/news/wonk/wp/2014/06/20/taxi-medallions-have-been-the-best-investment-in-america-for-years-now-uber-may-be-changing-that/.

23 Badger, https://www.washingtonpost.com/news/wonk/wp/2014/06/20/taxi-medallions-have-been-the-best-investment-in-america-for-years-now-uber-may-be-changing-that/.

24 Badger, https://www.washingtonpost.com/news/wonk/wp/2014/06/20/taxi-medallions-have-been-the-best-investment-in-america-for-years-now-uber-may-be-changing-that/.

25 Eric Newcomer, "Uber Pushed the Limits of the Law. Now Comes the Reckoning," *Bloomberg*, October 11, 2017, https://www.bloomberg.com/news/features/2017-10-11/uber-pushed-the-limits-of-the-law-now-comes-the-reckoning.

26 Michael King, "Lege for Sale? Uber and Lyft splurge on lobby to deregulate themselves," *The Austin Chronicle*, March 14, 2017, https://www.austinchronicle.com/daily/news/2017-03-14/lege-for-sale/.

27 Newcomer, Uber Pushed the Limits of the Law," https://www.bloomberg.com/news/features/2017-10-11/uber-pushed-the-limits-of-the-law-now-comes-the-reckoning.

Chapter 6

1   Jessica Mitford, *The American Way of Death Revisited* (New York: Knopf Doubleday Publishing Group, 2011), 31.

2   Richard Carleton Hacker, "Summer Spirits 2015," *Cigar World Magazine*, n.d., accessed July 13, 2020, https://old.cigarworld.com/cw-magazine/summer-spirits-2015/.

3   Laphraoig Whiskey (@Laphroaig), "We agree that #Laphroaig tastes like a medicine cabinet was lit on fire but it's not just for Vikings. #Scotch #OpinionsWelcome," Twitter post, February 16, 2018, https://twitter.com/Laphroaig/status/964624188400128001.

4   Vince Mancini, "A Near-Literal Crash Course in Scotch on the Isle of Jura," UP-ROXX, May 31, 2018, https://uproxx.com/life/jura-scotch-whisky/.

5   Press Release Businesswire, "The World's Best-Selling Islay Single Malt Scotch Whiskey, Laphroaig®, Prepares to Welcome Royal Guests and Residents of Islay as Friends," *Business Insider*, May 29, 2008, https://markets.businessinsider.com/news/stocks/the-world-s-best-selling-islay-single-malt-scotch-whisky-laphroaig-r-prepares-to-welcome-royal-guests-and-residents-of-islay-as-friends-1023992099#.

6   Eric Layer, "Product Marketing: Exclusivity Doesn't Always Mean a Big Price Tag," MarketingProfs, October 19, 2016, http://www.marketingprofs.com/opinions/2016/30935/product-marketing-exclusivity-doesnt-always-mean-a-big-price-tag.

7   "Google Entices Job-Searchers with Math Puzzle," *NPR Morning Edition*, September 14, 2004, https://www.npr.org/templates/story/story.php?storyId=3916173.

8   Layer, "Product Marketing," http://www.marketingprofs.com/opinions/2016/30935/product-marketing-exclusivity-doesnt-always-mean-a-big-price-tag.

9   Steve McKee, *Power Branding: Leveraging the Success of the World's Best Brands* (London: Palgrave Macmillan Publishing Company, 2014), 11.

10   Jonathan Salem Baskin, "According To U.S. Big Data, We Won The Vietnam War," *Forbes*, July 24, 2014, https://www.forbes.com/sites/jonathansalembaskin/2014/07/25/according-to-big-data-we-won-the-vietnam-war/#3005640a3f21. See also Charles Mohr, "McNamara on Record, Reluctantly, on Vietnam," *The New York Times*, May 16, 1984, https://www.forbes.com/sites/jonathansalembaskin/2014/07/25/according-to-big-data-we-won-the-vietnam-war.

11   Tim Williams, "What Replaces Timesheets," Ignition Consulting Group, accessed July 13, 2020, https://www.ignitiongroup.com/propulsion-blog/what-replaces-timesheets.

12   William Bruce Cameron, *Informal Sociology: A Casual Introduction to Sociological Thinking* (New York: Random House, 1963), 13.

13   Marcus Gattrell, "Designed Where Function Meets Fashion Then Punches It in the Face," MarcusGattrell.com/Carhartt, accessed June 12, 2020, https://bit.ly/3hn1yAO.

14   The exact budget figure varies depending on the definition of "advertising." *Ad Age* estimates P&G spent $7.1 billion on TV, print, radio, and internet and in-store ads between July 2017 and June 2018. However, by a broader definition, they estimate P&G spent nearly $10.5 billion in 2018. See Bradley Johnson, "Samsung Overtakes P&G

as World's Largest Advertiser," *Ad Age*, December 3, 2018, https://adage.com/article/news/global-marketers-2018-tktk/315743. AdBrands states that P&G's self-reported ad expenditure in 2019 was $6.75 billion. See "Procter & Gamble advertising & marketing profile," AdBrands.net, accessed July 13, 2020, https://www.adbrands.net/us/procter-and-gamble-us.htm.

15 Marielle Wakim, "The Amazing, True Story of How Nancy Silverton Became a Living Food Legend," *Los Angeles Magazine*, April 26, 2018, https://www.lamag.com/digestblog/nancy-silverton/. See also Chef's Table, season 3, episode 3, created by David Gelb, directed by Andrew Fried, available on Netflix.

16 Aaron Franklin, "Aaron Franklin Teaches Texas-Style BBQ, Official Trailer, Masterclass," YouTube video, MasterClass YouTube channel, uploaded May 16, 2019, 1:46, https://www.youtube.com/watch?v=IKpnD2BnwOU.

17 Steve McKee, *When Growth Stalls: How It Happens, Why You're Stuck, and What to Do About It* (Hoboken, NJ: John Wiley and Sons, 2009), 68-69.

18 McKee, *When Growth Stalls*, 68-69.

Chapter 7

1 Cited in Jessica Mitford, *The American Way of Death Revisited* (New York: Knopf Doubleday Publishing Group, 2011), 20.

2 Adam Andrzejewski, "Should Non-Profit U.S. Food Bank Executives Earn Nearly $1 Million Per Year?," *Forbes*, June 11, 2020, https://www.forbes.com/sites/adamandrzejewski/2020/06/11/should-non-profit-us-food-bank-executives-earn-up-to-11-million-per-year.

3 Jessica Silver-Greenberg, Jesse Drucker, and David Enrich, "Hospitals Got Bailouts and Furloughed Thousands While Paying C.E.O.s Millions," *The New York Times*, June 8, 2020, https://www.nytimes.com/2020/06/08/business/hospitals-bailouts-ceo-pay.html.

4 Armen Keteyian, "Greg Mortensen Could Face $20 Million in Back Taxes," *CBS News*, April 20, 2011, http://www.cbsnews.com/stories/2011/04/20/eveningnews/main20055865.shtml.

5 Lisa Chiu, "Mass. May Soon Ban Pay for Trustees of Nonprofit Groups," *The Chronicle of Philanthropy*, June 26, 2011, https://www.philanthropy.com/article/Mass-May-Soon-Ban-Pay-for/158219. See also Lisa Chiu, "Mass. Foundations Consider Proposed Restriction on Board-Member Pay," *The Chronicle of Philanthropy*, June 7, 2011, https://www.philanthropy.com/article/Mass-Foundations-Consider/227329.

6 Jessica Mitford, *The American Way of Death Revisited* (New York: Knopf Doubleday Publishing Group, 2011), 20.

7 Anonymous interviewee, Death Care Focus Group 2, McKee Wallwork + Co., April 1, 2019, Albuquerque, NM, Scribie transcript.

8 Bill Fish, "Best Online Mattress," SleepFoundation.org, updated June 30, 2020, https://www.sleepfoundation.org/best-mattress/best-online-mattress.

9   Jasmine Wu, "There are now 175 online mattress companies—and you can't tell them apart," *CNBC*, August 18, 2019, https://www.cnbc.com/2019/08/18/there-are-now-175-online-mattress-companiesand-you-cant-tell-them-apart.html.

10 Wu, https://www.cnbc.com/2019/08/18/there-are-now-175-online-mattress-companiesand-you-cant-tell-them-apart.html.

11 McKee Wallwork + Co., *Death Care Consumer Segmentation Study*, Banner 1, Q37_16, 157, and Q37_5, 135, unpublished report, August 2011, Microsoft Word document.

12 Perianne Boring, "Death Of The Death Care Industry And Eternal Life Online," *Forbes*, April 25, 2014, https://www.forbes.com/sites/perianneboring/2014/04/25/the-death-of-the-death-care-industry-and-eternal-life-online/.

13 National Funeral Directors Association (NFDA), 2019 *Consumer Awareness and Preferences Study* (April 2019), PowerPoint summary, 42, https://qhi7a3oj76cn9awl3qc-qrh3o-wpengine.netdna-ssl.com/wp-content/uploads/2020/02/Funeral-Directors-survey.pdf.

14 NFDA, 32, https://qhi7a3oj76cn9awl3qcqrh3o-wpengine.netdna-ssl.com/wp-content/uploads/2020/02/Funeral-Directors-survey.pdf.

15 Gary Laderman, *Rest in Peace: A Cultural History of Death and the Funeral Home in Twentieth-Century America* (Oxford: Oxford University Press, 2005), 99.

16 Laderman, 101.

17 Laderman, xxii.

18 Laderman, 99.

19 Funeral Service Foundation, *Thoughts and Feelings About Traditional Funerals and Your End of Life Ceremony* (Olson Zaltman Associates, August 2012), PowerPoint presentation, 63, http://www.cremationsolutions.com/blog/wp-content/uploads/2014/11/Funeral-Foundation-Study.pdf.

20 Funeral Service Foundation, 63, http://www.cremationsolutions.com/blog/wp-content/uploads/2014/11/Funeral-Foundation-Study.pdf.

21 *The Newsroom*, episode 1, "We Just Decided To," directed by Greg Mottola, written by Aaron Sorkin, aired June 24, 2012, on HBO. Dialogue excerpts available at *IMDb.com*, accessed July 16, 2020, https://www.imdb.com/title/tt2289479/characters/nm0001099.

22 Jessica Long, Chris Roark, and Bill Theofilou, *The Bottom Line on Trust: Achieve Competitive Agility* (Accenture, 2018), 4, https://www.accenture.com/_acnmedia/Thought-Leadership-Assets/PDF/Accenture-Competitive-Agility-Index.pdf.

23 Long, Roark, and Theofilou, 8, https://www.accenture.com/_acnmedia/Thought-Leadership-Assets/PDF/Accenture-Competitive-Agility-Index.pdf.

24 Long, Roark, and Theofilou, 10, https://www.accenture.com/_acnmedia/Thought-Leadership-Assets/PDF/Accenture-Competitive-Agility-Index.pdf.

25 Tor Myhren, "New eTrade Baby Barbershop," Grey New York, YouTube video, uploaded by GooN4190 on March 15, 2010, accessed August 9, 2020, https://www.youtube.com/watch?v=tndLAc7iQFw.

26 Alicia Adamczyk, "US airlines charged almost $5 billion in baggage fees last year—here's how to avoid them," *CNBC make it*, May 16, 2019, https://www.cnbc.com/2019/05/15/us-airlines-brought-in-almost-5-billion-dollars-in-baggage-fees-last-year.html.

27 "How Is Southwest Different From Other Airlines?," Investopedia, May 22, 2020, https://www.investopedia.com/articles/investing/061015/how-southwest-different-other-airlines.asp. See also Lou Whiteman, "Southwest Airlines Says It Has Two Years' Worth of Cash on Hand," The Motley Fool, June 17, 2020, https://www.fool.com/investing/2020/06/17/southwest-airlines-says-it-has-two-years-worth-of.aspx.

28 Kirsten Chang, "Battle for client assets heats up as brokers cut fees to zero," *CNBC*, October 14, 2019, https://www.cnbc.com/2019/10/13/battle-for-client-assets-heats-up-as-brokers-cut-fees-to-zero.html.

Chapter 8

1 "New Study Shows Americans Recognize the Role of Memorialization in Healthy Healing Following the Death of a Loved One," Funeral and Memorial Information Council, April 2015, accessed July 21, 2020, https://www.famic.org/famic-study/.

2 "Americans Recognize the Role of Memorialization," FAMIC, accessed July 21, 2020, https://www.famic.org/famic-study/.

3 Ben Hunt-Davis and Harriet Beveridge, *Will It Make the Boat Go Faster?: Olympic-Winning Strategies for Everyday Success* (Kibworth, UK: Troubador Publishing Ltd., 2020).

4 Robert Lea, "'Every company in the world is dying, the trick is knowing what to do next," *The Times*, April 22, 2017, https://www.thetimes.co.uk/article/every-company-in-the-world-is-dying-the-trick-is-knowing-what-to-do-next-qmgqmzzq0.

5 Simon London, Mike Useem, and Rodney Zemmel, "Leading for the Long Term," McKinsey & Company, June 15, 2018, podcast transcript, https://www.mckinsey.com/business-functions/strategy-and-corporate-finance/our-insights/leading-for-the-long%20term.

6 Nassim Nicholas Taleb, *Antifragile: Things that Gain from Disorder* (New York: Random House Trade Paperbacks, 2014), 3.

7 Rory McDonald and Kathleen Eisenhardt, "The New-Market Conundrum: In emerging industries the usual rules of strategy don't apply," *Harvard Business Review* (May-June 2020): 7.

Chapter 9

1 Bobby J. Calder, "Marketing Research and Understanding Consumers," in *Kellogg on Marketing*, ed. Alice M. Tybout and Bobby J. Calder, 2nd ed. (Hoboken, NJ: John Wiley and Sons Publishing, 2010), 63.

2 *Lexico*, s.v. "Psychographics," Oxford University Press, accessed July 26, 2020, https://www.lexico.com/en/definition/psychographics.

3 Maggie Jones, "The Movement to Bring Death Closer," *The New York Times Magazine*, December 19, 2020, updated January 13, 2020, https://www.nytimes.com/2019/12/19/magazine/home-funeral.html.

4 See "About Yum! Brands," Yum! Brands (website), accessed July 26, 2020, https://www.yum.com/wps/portal/yumbrands/Yumbrands/company.

5 "Latest Innovations: Smell Like a Man, Man," Procter & Gamble (factsheet), accessed July 25, 2020, https://www.pg.com/en_US/downloads/innovation/factsheet_Old-Spice.pdf.

6 Patricia Winters Lauro, "The Media Business: Advertising; Wassup? America's Asking," *The New York Times*, February 16, 2001, https://www.nytimes.com/2001/02/16/business/the-media-business-advertising-whassup-america-s-asking.html.

7 "Top 20 Slogans; 02: Nike (1987) – Just Do It, Dan Wieden, Wieden + Kennedy," *Creative Review*, accessed July 25, 2020, https://www.creativereview.co.uk/just-do-it-slogan/.

8 "The Ford F-Series is the best-selling vehicle in the world this year," *Fox News*, August 17, 2017, https://www.foxnews.com/auto/the-ford-f-series-is-the-best-selling-vehicle-in-the-world-this-year.

9 Transportation Research Center at Argonne National Library, "U.S. HEV Sales by Model," U.S Department of Energy, last updated January 2020, https://afdc.energy.gov/data/10301.

10 Ashley Rodriguez, "How Allstate's Mayhem Disrupted the Chatter Around Insurance - Marketer's Playbook: Destructive Character Helps 'In Good Hands' Stand Out," *AdAge*, June 10, 2015, https://adage.com/article/cmo-strategy/mayhem-helped-allstate-disrupt-conversation-insurance/298779.

11 Jim Edwards, "'Mayhem' Seems to Be Working Out Nicely for Allstate," *CBSNews*, January 11, 2011, https://www.cbsnews.com/news/mayhem-seems-to-be-working-out-nicely-for-allstate/.

12 AllState Insurance, "Cat :30, AllState Mayhem," YouTube video, AllState YouTube channel, uploaded September 12, 2019, https://www.youtube.com/watch?v=dHXL8A1dowo.

13 AllState Insurance, "Mayhem Teenage Girl," iSpotTV.com, accessed July 25, 2020, https://www.ispot.tv/ad/7kaG/allstate-featuring-mayhem-teenage-girl.

14 AllState Insurance, "Racoon Mayhem," YouTube video, uploaded by bnditlk7 on August 26, 2011, accessed July 25, 2020, https://www.youtube.com/watch?v=07h2O496kyU.

15 Evan Tarver, "Why the 'Share a Coke' Campaign Is So Successful," Investopedia, September 24, 2019, https://www.investopedia.com/articles/markets/100715/what-makes-share-coke-campaign-so-successful.asp.

16 "About Us: #LikeAGirl: How It All Started," Always.com, accessed July 25, 2020, https://always.com/en-us/about-us/likeagirl-how-it-all-started.

17 Ethan Wolff-Mann, "Why Dos Equis' 'Most Interesting Man' Ad Campaign Was So Successful," *Time Magazine*, March 9, 2016, https://time.com/4252403/enums/.

18 Falon Fatemi, "3 Tips to Empower your Sales Team, Inspired by Top Sales Organizations," *Forbes*, June 27, 2019, https://www.forbes.com/sites/falonfatemi/2019/06/27/3-tips-to-empower-your-sales-team-inspired-by-top-sales-organizations.

19 Micah Solomon, "Your Customer Service Is Your Branding: The Ritz-Carlton Case Study," *Forbes*, September 24, 2015, https://www.forbes.com/sites/micahsolomon/2015/09/24/your-customer-service-style-is-your-brand-the-ritz-carlton-case-study.

20 Steve McKee, *Power Branding: Leveraging the Success of the World's Best Brands* (London: Palgrave Macmillan Publishing Company, 2014), 14.

21 Kim Peterson, "12 things about Costco that may surprise you," *CBSNews*, July 16, 2014, https://www.cbsnews.com/media/12-things-about-costco-that-may-surprise-you/.

22 Danny Klein, "America's 34 Most Lucrative Fast-Food Chains," *QSR Magazine*, December 2019, accessed July 25, 2020, https://www.qsrmagazine.com/content/americas-34-most-lucrative-fast-food-chains.

23 Chloe Sorvino, "Exclusive: In-N-Out Billionaire Lynsi Snyder Opens Up About Her Troubled Past And The Burger Chain's Future," *Forbes*, October 10, 2018, https://www.forbes.com/sites/chloesorvino/2018/10/10/exclusive-in-n-out-billionaire-lynsi-snyder-opens-up-about-her-troubled-past-and-the-burger-chains-future/.

Chapter 10

1 Jason Dedrick, Kenneth L. Kraemer, and Tony Tsai, *Acer: An IT Company Learning to Use Information* (Irvine, CA: Center for Research on Information Technology and Organization, University of California, Irvine, 1999), 7, https://escholarship.org/uc/item/9j8146rq.

2 Tim Williams, "Professional Firms Provide Value the Same Way Pilots Do," LinkedIn Pulse, June 5, 2018, https://www.linkedin.com/pulse/professional-firms-should-earn-money-way-pilots-do-tim-williams/.

3 Microsoft, "Reinvented Around You," iSpot.tv, aired November 11, 2012-December 17, 2012, accessed August 9, 2020, https://www.ispot.tv/ad/77s5/microsoft-windows-phone-reinvented-around-you?conv=1.

4 Microsoft, "Windows Phone 7 advert 2010" ["Really?!"], YouTube video, uploaded by Computastar Ltd. on February 27, 2010, accessed August 9, 2020, https://www.youtube.com/watch?v=zNKz6dAH2Wo. Emphasis added.

5 S. O'Dea, "Windows Phone OS market share of smartphone shipments worldwide from 1st quarter 2011 to 4th quarter 2016," *Statista*, February 27, 2020, https://www.statista.com/statistics/236034/global-smartphone-os-market-share-of-windows-mobile/.

6 Apple, "iPhone 4 Apple 'FaceTime' 2010 Commercial," YouTube video, uploaded by CommercialsUSA on July 13, 2010, accessed August 9, 2020, https://www.youtube.com/watch?v=TmE6jrqqsQQ.

7 Statista Research Department, "Smartphone market share of Apple and Samsung in the United States from 1st quarter 2010 to 1st quarter 2012," Statista, August 8, 2012, https://www.statista.com/statistics/242388/market-share-of-smartphone-vendors-in-the-united-states-usa/.

8 See Chapter 1 and discussion of Jessica Mitford, *The American Way of Death Revisited* (New York: Knopf Doubleday Publishing Group, 2011).

9 Patrick M. Lencioni, *Getting Naked: A Business Fable About Shedding the Three Fears That Sabotage Client Loyalty* (Hoboken, NJ: John Wiley & Sons, 2010), 201.

10 Maggie Jones, "The Movement to Bring Death Closer," *The New York Times Magazine*, December 19, 2019, updated January 13, 2020, https://www.nytimes.com/2019/12/19/magazine/home-funeral.html.

11 Paul Lopushinsky, "Why Akio Morita, Co-Founder of Sony, Is One of My Product Manager Heroes, and Why he should be yours as well," Medium.com, March 7, 2017, https://medium.com/open-product-management/why-akio-morita-co-founder-of-sony-is-one-of-my-product-manager-heroes-and-why-he-should-be-783bebee82c7.

12 "How It Works," DIRTT (company website), accessed July 29, 2020, https://www.dirtt.com/how-it-works/.

13 Camilla Cornell, "How DIRTT has built a successful green manufacturing business in Calgary," *Financial Post*, April 8, 2013, https://financialpost.com/entrepreneur/how-dirtt-has-built-a-successful-green-manufacturing-business-in-calgary.

14 Bracken Hendricks and Matt Golden, "Taking on the Tool Belt Recession: Energy Efficiency Retrofits Can Provide a Real Help for Construction Unemployment," Center for American Progress, March 3, 2010, https://www.americanprogress.org/issues/green/reports/2010/03/03/7442/taking-on-the-tool-belt-recession/.

Chapter 11

1 Cyril Northcote Parkinson, Parkinson's Law and Other Studies in Administration (Cambridge, MA: Riverside Press, 1957), 26.

2 Seamus Sweeney, "Beware the gleaming, purpose built headquarters: C. Northcote Parkinson's Law of Buildings," Seamussweeney.net, May 31, 2019, https://seamussweeney.net/2019/05/31/beware-the-gleaming-purpose-built-headquarters-c-northcote-parkinsons-law-of-buildings/.

3 Sweeney, https://seamussweeney.net/2019/05/31/beware-the-gleaming-purpose-built-headquarters-c-northcote-parkinsons-law-of-buildings/.

4 John Milton, Paradise Lost, bk. 1, lines 200-208, The John Milton Reading Room, Dartmouth University, accessed August 4, 2020, https://www.dartmouth.edu/~milton/reading_room/pl/book_1/text.shtml.

5 "The last Kodak moment?" *The Economist*, January 14, 2014, https://www.economist.com/business/2012/01/14/the-last-kodak-moment. See also Claudia H. Deutsch, "At Kodak, Some Old Things Are New Again," The New York Times, May 2, 2008, https://www.nytimes.com/2008/05/02/technology/02kodak.html.

6   David Usborne, "The moment it all went wrong for Kodak," *Independent*, January 20, 2012, https://www.independent.co.uk/news/business/analysis-and-features/the-moment-it-all-went-wrong-for-kodak-6292212.html.

7   Marc Randolph, "He 'was struggling not to laugh': Inside Netflix's crazy, doomed meeting with Blockbuster," *Vanity Fair*, September 17, 2019, https://www.vanityfair.com/news/2019/09/netflixs-crazy-doomed-meeting-with-blockbuster.

8   Matt Phillips and Roberto A. Ferdman, "A brief, illustrated history of Blockbuster, which is closing the last of its US stores," *Quartz*, November 6, 2013, https://qz.com/144372/a-brief-illustrated-history-of-blockbuster-which-is-closing-the-last-of-its-us-stores/.

9   Catherine Clifford, "How Amazon founder Jeff Bezos went from the son of a teen mom to the world's richest person," CNBC, October 27, 2017, https://www.cnbc.com/2017/10/27/how-amazon-founder-jeff-bezos-went-from-the-son-of-a-teen-mom-to-the-worlds-richest-person.html.

10 Robert Kyncl, "The inside story of how Netflix transitioned to digital video after seeing the power of YouTube," *Vox*: Recode, September 13, 2017, https://www.vox.com/2017/9/13/16288364/streampunks-book-excerpt-youtube-netflix-pivot-video.

11 David Robertson and Bill Breen, Brick by Brick: How LEGO Rewrote the Rules of Innovation and Conquered the Global Toy Industry (New York: Harper Collins Publishing, 2014), 108-109.

Epilogue

Jessica Mitford, *The American Way of Death Revisited* (New York: Knopf Doubleday Publishing Group, 2011), pp. xi, 3, 13-17, 64, 66, 141, 142, 149.

Index

CPSIA information can be obtained
at www.ICGtesting.com
Printed in the USA
LVHW082039121121
703199LV00002B/5/J